COLUMBIA

ENGLISH

GRAMMAR

FOR **GMAT** ®

WITH ANSWERS

**A SCORE-RAISING GMAT GRAMMAR
BOOK FOR ADVANCED STUDENTS**

Richard Lee, Ph.D.

COLUMBIA PRESS

To Nancy, Philip, and Christina

CONTENTS

TO THE STUDENT

Chapter 3 NOUN CLAUSES

Chapter 4 ADJECTIVE CLAUSES

Chapter 5 ADVERB CLAUSES

Chapter 6 PARALLEL STRUCTURES

Chapter 7 CONDITIONAL SENTENCES AND WISHES

Chapter 8 MODALS AND MODAL-LIKE VERBS

Chapter 9 MODIFIERS AND DANGLING PARTICIPLES

Chapter 10 PRONOUN AND PRONOUN REFERENCES

Chapter 11 VERBALS

Chapter 12 COMPARATIVES AND SUPERLATIVES

To the Student

COLUMBIA ENGLISH GRAMMAR FOR GMAT is written for students who need some extra help with English grammar and usage. It covers all the absolutely essential grammar points, such as subject-verb agreement, dangling modifier, parallel structure, and others that are most often tested on the GMAT. It is the only self-study reference and practice book that you will ever need to raise your score on the test.

HERE IS WHAT YOU WILL GET:

- **ERROR EXAMPLES:** show you what kinds of mistakes most often made at GMAT and how to correct them;
- **GRAMMAR POINTS:** teach you all the English grammar and usage you need to know for the test;
- **PRACTICE TESTS:** Use sample Sentence Correction and Sentence Completion questions to test your grammar power and readiness for the real GMAT;
- **ANSWER KEYS:** provide answers and explanations to help you avoid the mistakes forever.

COLUMBIA ENGLISH GRAMMAR FOR GMAT gives you an English professor's proven method, guaranteed to help you master all the essential grammar and usage for the test. It is a must-have English grammar book that will help you to ace the GMAT!

CHAPTER 1

SUBJECT-VERB
AGREEMENT

LESSON 1

PROBLEMS WITH SUBJECT

AND VERB AGREEMENT

ERROR EXAMPLE

WRONG: The motorcycle, like other two-wheeled vehicles, are more
dangerous than vehicles having four wheels.

RIGHT: The **motorcycle**, like other two-wheeled vehicles, **is** more
dangerous than vehicles having four wheels.

GRAMMAR POINT

In English, a sentence must have a subject and verb, and they have to agree in number.

Gloria is the most charming girl in our school.

The new **iPhones cost** more money than the previous models.

Jack studies Chinese as a second language.

In the first example, *Gloria* is the third person singular; therefore, the linking verb *is* is in the third person singular. In the second example, **iPhones** is the plural form; therefore, the action verb *cost* should be in the plural form. In the third example, *Jack* is the third person singular, therefore, the action verb *studies* is in the third person singular.

Despite the fact that it is hard to deal with all kinds of problems with the subject and verb agreement, we have to pay special attention to the following two types of mistakes we often make with subject and verb agreement:

1. A third person singular verb is used with the plural subject or vice versa.

WRONG: Her mother and sister is coming to American to attend my convocation.

RIGHT: Her **mother and sister are** coming to American to attend my convocation.

WRONG: Mathematics have been the most difficult subject this semester.

RIGHT: **Mathematics has been** the most difficult subject this

semester.

In the first example, her *mother and sister* together make a plural subject, therefore, the linking verb be should be in the plural form: *are*. In the second example, mathematics is a singular noun; therefore, the verb should be in the third person singular form: *has been*.

2. A subject with phrases or clauses is separated from the verb.

WRONG: Our dog, one of my wife's favorite pets, enjoy the most special treatment in our house.

RIGHT: Our **dog**, one of my wife's favorite pets, **enjoys** the most special treatment in our house.

WRONG: Hong Kong, the shopping paradise for tourists, are truly the place for bargain hunters.

RIGHT: **Hong Kong**, the shopping paradise for tourists, **is** truly the

place for bargain hunters.

In the first example, *one of my wife's favorite pets* is the appositive of our *dog*, therefore, the subject is still third person singular and a singular verb *enjoys* should be used. In the second example, the shopping paradise for tourists is the appositive of Hong Kong, therefore, the subject *Hong Kong* is still singular, a third person singular verb *is* should be used.

PRACTICE TEST

Test 1. SENTENCE COMPLETION: Choose the CORRECT answer.

1. Clinton Westwood, accompanied by his body guards,
   _____warmly welcomed in Shanghai.

   A. were

   B. was

2. The number of international students _____every year in
   our university.

   A. is increasing

   B. are increasing

3. New York City, the paradise on earth, _____the most
   tourists in the world.

   A. attract

   B. attracts

4. Either your answer or your classmates' answers
   _____acceptable to me.

   A. are

   B. is

5. Neither Michael nor Christine_____to hold late night
   parties in this building.

A. are allowed

B. is allowed

2. Test. SENTENCE CORRECTION: Choose the INCORRECT word or phrase and CORRECT it.

1. One of his uncles are professor of English at Princeton University.

2. Either his brother or sisters is from England.

3. A number of students is considered for fellowships this year.

4. Neither my parents nor my sister are happy about my not going to college.

5. The committee is willing vote for his appointment.

ANSWER KEY

Test 1:

1. B

2. A

3. B

4. A

5. B (Here you should use *is allowed;* for the verb must agree in number and in person with the closest noun or pronoun when we use *neither...nor/either...or* structures.)

Test 2:

1. **One** of his uncles **is** professor of English at Princeton University.

2. Either his brother or **sisters are** from England.

3. A number of **students are** considered for fellowships this year.

4. Neither my parents nor my **sister is** happy about my not going to college.

5. The **committee are** willing vote for his appointment.

LESSON 2

FAULTY SUBJECT-VERB AGREEMENT: MODIFIED SUBJECT AND VERB

ERROR EXAMPLE

WRONG: In Washington, DC, the FBI Scientific Crime Detection Laboratory, better known as the FBI Crime Lab facilities, officially open.

RIGHT: In Washington, DC, the FBI Scientific Crime Detection **Laboratory**, better known as the FBI Crime Lab facilities, officially **opens**.

GRAMMAR POINT

A sentence must have a subject and a verb. In all patterns, the subject and the verb must agree in person and in number. Never use a verb that agrees with the modifier of a subject instead of with a subject itself.

The Zoning Improvement **Plan,** better known as zip codes, **helps** postal clerks to do their work more effectively.

Everyone who had the opportunity to work beside the President and his cabinet **was** impressed by his vision and leadership.

Either of these buses **goes** past College Park.

PRACTICE TEST

Test 1. SENTENCE COMPLETION: Choose the CORRECT answer.

1. All those students who have handed in their term papers_____allowed to go home.

   A. was

   B. were

2. Washington D.C., the capital of the United States, _____the political and cultural centre of the country.

A. is known as

B. are known as

3. Gordon Campbell, the star of all stars, _____nominated to receive the President's Medal.

A. was

B. were

4. Neither of the alternatives that had been outlined at the last meeting _____the executive committee.

A. were acceptable to

B. was acceptable to

5. Nobody who was near the scene of the crime _____.

A. is above suspicion

B. are above suspicion

2. Test. SENTENCE CORRECTION: Choose the INCORRECT word or phrase and CORRECT it.

1. His knowledge of languages and international relations aid him in *aids* his work.

2. The facilities at the new research library, including an excellent microfilm file, is among the best in the country. *are*

3. All trade between the two countries were suspended pending negotiation of a new agreement.

4. The production of different kinds of artificial materials are essential to the conservation of our natural resources.

5. Since the shipment of supplies for our experiments were delayed, we will have to reschedule our work.

ANSWER KEY

Test 1:

1. B ✓
2. A ✓
3. A ✓
4. B ✓
5. B ✓

Test 2:

1. His **knowledge** of languages and international relations **aids** him in his work.

2. The **facilities** at the new research library, including an excellent microfilm file, **are** among the best in the country.

3. All **trade** between the two countries **was** suspended pending negotiation of a new agreement.

4. The **production** of different kinds of artificial materials **is** essential to the conversation of our natural resources.

5. Since the **shipment** of supplies for our experiments **was** delayed, we will have to reschedule our work.

LESSON 3

FAULTY SUBJECT-VERB AGREEMENT: SUBJECT WITH ACCOMPANIMENT AND VERB

ERROR EXAMPLE

WRONG: The Hollywood actress, Mary Shelly, along with the likes of Jenny Middleton and Nancy Tea, were added to the best-dressed list of the New Fashion Magazine.

RIGHT: The Hollywood **actress**, Mary Shelly, along with the likes of Jenny Middleton and Nancy Tea, **was** added to the best-dressed list of the New Fashion Magazine.

GRAMMAR POINT

Remember that the subject and the verb of a sentence must agree in number and in person. Never use a verb that agrees with a phrase of accompaniment instead of with the subject itself.

The high protein **content** of various strains of alfalfa plants, along with the characteristically long root system that enable them to survive long droughts, **makes** them particularly valuable in arid countries.

The teen **beauty**, having been accepted by both Harvard and Yale, **was**

also offered a Port of Entry scholarship.

WRONG: This prize money, together with a little bit of common
           sense, were enough for the poor family.

RIGHT: This prize money, together with a little bit of common sense,
           was enough for the poor family.

PRACTICE TEST

Test 1. SENTENCE COMPLETION: Choose the CORRECT answer.

1. The farmer's boy, having been offered a scholarship to go to the University of Rochester, _____ immediately known to the whole country.

   A. were

   B. was

2. The Hollywood actress, guarded by twelve big men, _____into the Reception Hall.

A. was escorted

B. were

3. The small town., having a population of eighty-six people, _____the biggest stadium in the State.

A. have

B. has

4. The Big Cat, known as the Dragon Cat, _____eyes as big as car lamps.

A. have

B. has

5. Anyone who is not satisfied with our service_____entitled to receive a free coupon of five dollars.

A. is

B. are

2. Test. SENTENCE CORRECTION: Choose the INCORRECT word or phrase and CORRECT it.

1. The guest of honor, along with his wife and two sons, was [~~were~~] seated at the first table.

2. The ambassador, with his family and staff, invites [invite] you to

a reception at the embassy on Tuesday afternoon at five

o'clock.

3. Mary, accompanied by her brother on the piano, ~~were~~ was very well received at the talent show.

4. Senator MacDonald, with his assistant and his press secretary, ~~are~~ is scheduled to arrive in New York today.

5. Bruce Springsteen, accompanied by the E. Street Band, ~~are~~ is appearing in concert at the Student Center on Saturday night.

ANSWER KEY

Test 1:

1. B

2. A

3. B

4. B

5. A

Test 2:

1. **The guest of honor**, along with his wife and two sons, **was** seated at the first table.

2. **The ambassador**, with his family and staff, **invites** you to a reception at the embassy on Tuesday afternoon at five o'clock.

3. **Mary**, accompanied by her brother on the piano, **was** very well received at the talent show.

4. **Senator MacDonald**, with his assistant and his press secretary, **is** scheduled to arrive in New York today

5. **Bruce Springsteen**, accompanied by the E. Street Band, **is** appearing in concert at the Student Center on Saturday night.

LESSON 4

FAULTY SUBJECT-VERB AGREEMENT: SUBJECT WITH APPOSITIVE AND VERB

ERROR EXAMPLE

WRONG: The Emperor, father of ninety children, were living a very extravagant life.

RIGHT: The **Emperor,** father of ninety children, **was** living a very extravagant life.

GRAMMAR POINT

The subject and the verb in a sentence must agree in person and in number. An appositive is a word or phrase that follows a noun and defines it. It usually has a comma before it and a comma after it.

Remember: never use a verb that agrees with words in the appositive after a subject instead of with the subject itself.

Victoria, the capital of the Province of British Columbia , **is** not only one of the most beautiful cities in the world but also a university city with the most international students.

Dream Land, the hidden valley in the Cypress Mountains, **is** the only place in the world where dreams come true.

WRONG: Cindy, my colleague, are working for the National Research Institute.

RIGHT: Cindy, my colleague, **is working** for the National Research Institute.

PRACTICE TEST

Test 1. SENTENCE COMPLETION: Choose the CORRECT answer.

1. Cypress National Park, the free ski resort, _____the best possible facilities you can ever imagine.

(A.) has

B. have

2. Vancouver Island, the Island of Whales, _____ only two hours away from Vancouver by ferry.

(A. is)

B. are

3. Richard Wilson, famous author of more than eighty books,_____ a reputation of smoking only Cuban cigars.

A. have

(B. has)

4. The beautiful English professor, the queen of romance, _____ recently nominated to receive the Nobel Prize.

(A. was)

B. were

5. Yellow Lake City, the birthplace of the famous poet, _____ now become a major tourist spot in the country.

A. have

(B. has)

2. Test. SENTENCE CORRECTION: Choose the INCORRECT word or phrase and CORRECT it.

1. The books, an English dictionary and a chemistry textbook,

were

(was) on the bookshelf yesterday.

2. Three swimmers from our team, Paul, Edward, and Jim ~~is~~ *one* in competition for medals.

3. Several pets, two dogs and a cat, ~~needs~~ *need* to be taken care of while we are gone.

4. The Empire State University, the largest of state-supported school, ~~have~~ *has* more than 50,000 students on its main campus.

5. This recipe, an old family secret, ~~are~~ *is* an especially important part of our holiday celebrations.

ANSWER KEY

Test 1:

1. A

2. A

3. B

4. A

5. B

Test 2:

1. **The books**, an English dictionary and a chemistry textbook, **were** on the bookshelf yesterday.

2. **Three swimmers** from our team, Paul, Edward, and Jim, **are** in competition for medals.

3. **Several pets**, two dogs and a cat, **need** to be taken care of while we are gone.

4. **The Empire State University**, the largest of state-supported school, **has** more than 50,000 students on its main campus.

5. **This recipe**, an old family secret, **is** an especially important part of our holiday celebrations.

LESSON 5

FAULTY SUBJECT AND VERB AGREEMENT: INDEFINITE SUBJECT AND VERB

ERROR EXAMPLE

WRONG: Each of the radioisotopes produced artificially have its own distinct structure.

RIGHT: **Each** of the radioisotopes produced artificially **has** its own distinct structure.

GRAMMAR POINT

In English, when the following pronouns are used as indefinite subjects, they must be followed by singular verbs:

anyone	*either*	*neither*	*what*
anything	*everyone*	*no one*	*whatever*
each	*everything*	*nothing*	*whoever*

1. ANYONE

It's not a job for **anyone** who **is** slow with numbers.

If **anyone deserves** to be happy, you do.

2. EITHER

I will take this route if **either is** acceptable to you.

Either of the sisters **is** a beauty.

3. NEITHER

Neither of the brothers **is** good at school.

You are not allowed to smoke in this bar **neither is** your partner.

4. WHAT

What goes in will go out. Life is just a cycle.

What is done is undone.

5. ANYTHING

Mary asked: *"***Is anything** wrong?*"*

Anything that **is** expensive is not necessary good.

6. EVERYONE

Everyone in the street **was** shocked when they heard the news.

Not **everyone thinks** that the government is being particularly generous.

7. NO ONE

Everyone wants to be a hero, but **no one wants** to die.

No one knows for sure what will happen when the recession

continues.

8. WHATEVER

When you're older I think you're better equipped mentally to cope with **whatever happens**.

He will do **whatever pleases** her mother.

9. EACH

Each of them **is** right in this matter.

Each alternately **claims** it as its own.

10. EVERYTHING

Everything in this room **has** to be kept as it is while I am away.

Everything is going to be just fine.

11. NOTHING

Nothing is impossible in this world if you try hard enough.

There **is nothing** to worry about.

12. WHOEVER

Whoever says so, I don't believe it anyway.

You can give this iPad to **whoever wants** it. It's my gift.

The following subjects require either a singular or a plural verb depending on a qualifying phrase or other context from the sentence:

all   *any*   *some*   *the rest*

1. ALL

All of the money **has been spent**.

All of them **have gone** to Whistler for the weekend.

All is well that **ends** well.

2. ANY

Clean the mussels and discard **any** that **do not close**.

Is any of you from the West Coast?

3. SOME

The terrorized tourists had congregated in the only open bar in town. **Some were** very upset, but others looked as if nothing had happened.

Their research project is in trouble. **Some** more **money is** needed to keep it going.

4. THE REST

The **rest needs** no telling.

The rest of us are reprimanded for even the smallest transgression, while he can get away with murder.

PRACTICE TEST

Test 1. SENTENCE COMPLETION: Choose the CORRECT answer.

1. I have no doubt, neither_____he, that it was an encounter with God.

   A. do

   B. does

2. Any_____better than none.

   A. are

   B. is

3. Some of this material for some of you_____very difficult.

   A. is going to be

   B. are going to be

4. Neither of us_____aware of the fact that it was simply a lie.

A. were

B. was

5. Each student_____required to attend at least half of the total number of assembly meetings each term.

A. are

B. is

2. Test. SENTENCE CORRECTION: Choose the INCORRECT word or phrase and CORRECT it.

1. Everyone who has traveled across the United States by car, train, or bus are surprised to see such a large expanse of territory with such variation among the life-styles of the people.

2. Either of these trains go to Seattle over the weekend.

3. Anyone who wishes to participate in the state lottery have to

    purchase a ticket at a store that displays the official lottery seal.

4. The United States and Canada are close neighbors. Neither requires that the citizens of the other country have to apply for entry visas.

5. No one who majors in business is allowed to take courses at the School of Music this semester.

ANSWER KEY

Test 1:

1. B

2. B

3. A

4. B

5. B

Test 2:

1. **Everyone** who has traveled across the United States by car, train, or bus **is** surprised to see such a large expanse of territory with such variation among the life-styles of the people.

2. **Either** of these trains **goes** to Seattle over the weekend.

3. **Anyone** who wishes to participate in the state lottery **has** to purchase a ticket at a store that displays the official lottery seal.

4. The United States and Canada are close neighbors. **Neither requires** that the citizens of the other country have to apply for entry visas.

5. **No one** who majors in business **is** allowed to take courses at the School of Music this semester.

LESSON 6

FAULTY SUBJECT AND VERB AGREEMENT: COLLECTIVE SUBJECT AND VERB

ERROR EXAMPLE

WRONG: Because entertaining is such a competitive business, a group of singers or musicians need a manager to help market the music.

RIGHT: Because entertaining is such a competitive business, a **group** of singers or musicians **needs** a manager to help market the music.

GRAMMAR POINT

In English, some collective nouns used as collective subjects may cause problems with the subject verb agreement. The following is a list of the most common collective subjects (collective nouns) that must agree with singular verbs:

audience	*faculty*	*police*	*variety*
band	*family*	*public*	*2, 3, 4, ...dollars*
chorus	*group*	*series*	*2, 3, 4, ...miles*
class	*majority*	*staff*	*committee*
orchestra	*team*		

1. AUDIENCE

The **audience was** quite moved by his passionate speech.

The audience is invited to ask questions at the end.

2. FACULTY

The **faculty has agreed on** a change in the requirements.

But if the faculty finds out, I will have to leave Toronto.

3. POLICE

The **police has set up** a road block on Kingsway and Main Street.

The **police has** sufficient evidence to connect the suspect with the explosion.

4. VARIETY

This **variety** of dog **is** very useful for hunting.

Variety of methods **helps** to liven up a lesson.

5. BAND

The **band is** just back from a sell - out European tour.

The **band has been** on the road for almost two months.

6. FAMILY

The **family has traced** its ancestry to the Norman invaders.

Each **family** of gorillas **is** led by a great silverbacked patriarch.

7. PUBLIC

The **public has** to be educated to use resources more effectively.

The **public was** awakened to the full horror of the situation.

8. 1,2, 3 DOLLARS

A million dollars is not big sum for some terribly rich people.

Five dollars was too much for a bowl of rice.

9. CHORUS

The **chorus was** seated above the orchestra.

The **chorus was** singing the "The Ode of Joy."

10. GROUP

The singing **group is** under the direction of Mr. Johnson.

The army **group is** shipping out for the Far East today.

11. SERIES

The **series was** based on the autobiographies of the author.

In some people's view, TV **series is** a kind of quasi - art.

12. 2,3,4 MILES

Ten miles is not a short distance for a little girl who has to walk to school everyday.

A thousand miles is no longer a problem for traveller nowadays with the help of the airplane.

13. CLASS

The **class starts** in five minutes

Our **class has** twenty-five students from around the world.

14. MAJORITY

The **majority was** determined to press it proposal.

If the **majority decides** to pass the bill, the minorities will benefit the most.

15. STAFF

The **staff** of the school **is** one of the best in the city.

Our **staff is** always ready,willing,and able to help you.

16. COMMITTEE

The **committee was** unable to make a decision whether to fire its president or not.

I'm afraid the **committee has** cried your suggestion down.

17. ORCHESTRA

Our **orchestra deserves** ranking with the best in the world.

Under its new conductor, the **orchestra has established** an international reputation.

18. TEAM

The **team was** pointing for the game with the neighboring college.

Our **team was** left raging at the referee's decision.

To use the above collective subjects correctly, we must remember that never use a plural verb with a collect subject.

NOTE: In certain cases, if we express the separate nature of individuals in a group, a plural verb may be used with the collective subject (collective noun as subject):

The **police are** chasing the murder suspect on the highway now.

In this example, the *police* here is not meant as a *legal organization*, but as *police officers*, therefore, the plural verb can be used.

PRACTICE TEST

Test 1. SENTENCE COMPLETION: Choose the CORRECT answer.

1. The chorus_____very good today. Everybody loved it.

A. was

B. were

2. Such a group of formation_____briefly referred to as a transformation group.

A. are

B. is

3. The committee_____approved your request to go ahead with the project.

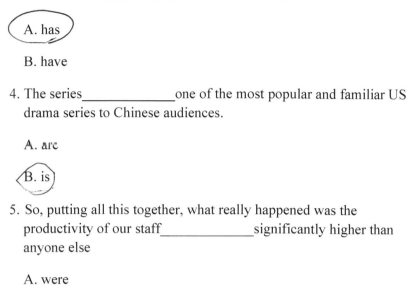

A. has

B. have

4. The series_____one of the most popular and familiar US drama series to Chinese audiences.

A. are

B. is

5. So, putting all this together, what really happened was the productivity of our staff_____significantly higher than anyone else

A. were

B. was

2. Test. SENTENCE CORRECTION: Choose the INCORRECT word or phrase and CORRECT it.

1. Twenty dollars are the price. *is*

2. Many people is coming to the graduation ceremony. *are*

3. An audience usually do not applaud in a church. *does*

4. Four miles are the distance to the office. *is*

5. The staff are meeting in the conference room. *is*

ANSWER KEY

Test 1:

1. A

2. B

3. A

4. B

5. B

Test 2:

1. **Twenty dollars *is*** the price.

2. **Many people *are coming*** to the graduation ceremony.

3. An **audience** usually ***does not applaud*** in a church.

4. **Four miles *is*** the distance to the office.

5. The **staff *is*** meeting in the conference room.

CHAPTER 2

VERB TENSES

LESSON 7

PROBLEMS WITH VERB

TENSE MEANINGS

ERROR EXAMPLE

WRONG: Americans found themselves with less free time over the past few decades even though they are earning more money.

RIGHT: Americans **have found** themselves with less free time over the past few decades even though they are earning more money.

GRAMMAR POINT

Different verb tense forms have different tense meanings. The following are the most common types of problems with verb tenses:

1. THE SIMPLE PAST TENSE:

We use the Simple Past Tense to express an event or situation that began and ended in the past.

> In 1992, Bill Clinton **became** President of the United States, beating his opponent by a wide margin.
>
> The old American couple finally **visited** Tibet last summer.
>
> After waiting for an hour for her boyfriend at the station, Mary **decided** to take the train alone to New York.
>
> WRONG: We have moved to New York City in 1989.
>
> RIGHT: We **moved** to New York City in 1989.

2. THE PRESENT PERFECT TENSE:

We use the Present Perfect Tense to give the idea that the action started in the past and still relates to the present. In other words, the action in the past has a result now.

> Michael **has** just **finished** his term paper after weeks of toiling in the library and at home.

I **have found** the letter you were looking for. Here you are, my dear friend.

I **haven't seen** Professor Lee Johnson for a long time.

WRONG: I lived in San Francisco since 1987.

RIGHT: I **have lived** in San Francisco since 1987.

3. THE PAST PERFECT TENSE:

We use the Past Perfect Tense to refer to a past situation or activity that had happened before another past situation or activity, or before a particular time in the past.

Joyce **had** just **eaten** dinner before her parents arrived at 7:30 last night.

The movie **had begun** by the time we got there.

By 2011, the United States **had** already **become** the No. 1 destination for international students.

WRONG: Philip have lived in Denver for ten years before he moved to the Silicon Valley to start his own company.

RIGHT: Philip **had lived** in Denver for ten years before he moved to the Silicon Valley to start his own company.

The meaning of a verb tense in a sentence must agree with the time meaning of the rest of the sentence. The time meaning of a sentence is often determined by words or expressions which we call *time markers*. The following are some of the most commonly used *TIME MARKERS*:

1. SINCE

We use *since* with the perfect tenses-to indicate a particular time.

Because National statistics on crime **have** only **been kept** *since* 1930, it is impossible to make judgments about crime during the early years of the nation.

2. FOR

We use *for* with the perfect tenses or the simple tenses to indicate a duration of time.

She **has been** in the U.S. *for* six months.

3. YET

We use *yet* with the perfect tenses-in negative meanings and in questions.

I have just got my acceptance letter from Yale University. **Have** you **heard** from Harvard University *yet*?

4. ALREADY

We use *already* with the perfect tenses-in affirmative meanings.

By the time I **got** to the airport, the plane **had *already* taken off**.

5. DURING

We use *during* with the simple and continuous tenses to show a duration of time. Not usually used with the perfect tenses.

Everybody **is having** a hard time *during* the recession.

PRACTICE TEST

Test 1. SENTENCE COMPLETION: Choose the CORRECT answer.

1. By September 2018, Jack Morgon will_____.

   A. graduate from Harvard Law School.

   B. have graduated from Harvard Law School.

2. In 2012, Clarissa_____Chairman of the Women's Rights International.

   A. had become

   B. became

3. These kinds of clothes_____ very popular in the countryside during the depression.

A. were

B. have been

4. When you called me last night, I_____ dinner with my parents.

A. was having

B. had had

5. They _____.five skyscrapers in Star City by the end of 2011.

A. already built.

B. had already built

Test 2. SENTENCE CORRECTION: Choose the INCORRECT word or phrase and CORRECT it.

1. By the time I got to the airport, the plane has already taken off. *had*

2. I traveled to five major cities since I cam to the United States last year. *have*

3. The ground is wet. It must rained. *have*

4. I took a shower when Helen called me last night. *was taking*

5. By the end of 2005 I have already finished my bachelor's degree in computer science at the University of Rochester. *had*

56

ANSWER KEY

Test 1:

1. B ✓

2. B (Here simple past tense should be used: *become;* for it refers to the action that began and ended in the past.)

3. A ✓

4. A ✓

5. B ✓

Test 2:

1. By the time I got to the airport, the plane **had** already **taken off**.

2. I **have traveled** to five major cities since I cam to the United States last year.

3. The ground is wet. It must **have rained**.

4. I **was taking** a shower when Helen called me last night.

5. By the end of 2005 I **had** already **finished** my bachelor's degree in computer science at the University of Rochester.

LESSON 8

USE *HAVE* + PAST PARTICIPLE AND *HAD* +PAST PARTICIPLE CORRECTLY

ERROR EXAMPLE

WRONG: After the votes were counted, it had been determined that Obama was the winner.

RIGHT : After the votes **had been counted**, it **was** determined that Obama was the winner.

GRAMMAR POINT

The Present Perfect Tense (*have* + past participle) and the Past Perfect Tense (*had* + past participle) are often confused. They have completely different uses, and we should learn to how to differentiate them.

1.THE PRESENT PERFECT TENSE: *HAVE* + PAST PARTICIPLE

The Present Perfect refers to an action or situation that started in the past and still relates to the present.

William Black **has lived** in Vancouver *for* almost twenty years.

Nowadays, Apple's iPhones **have become** a fashion among young

people in every part of the world..

Because her proposal **has been rejected**, she is very depressed.

She **has worked** very hard lately.

WRONG: By the time we got to the party, the guests have already
       left.

RIGHT : By the time we got to the party, the guests **had** already **left**.

2. THE PAST PERFECT TENSE: *HAD* + PAST PARTICIPLE

The Past Perfect refers to an activity or situation that took place before another past activity or situation.

We would have accomplished the task much earlier if you **had come** to help us.

Jennifer **had finished** her dinner when Jack came to pick her up.

Mary **had** already **gone** to sleep when we arrived at midnight.

By the end of the nineteenth century, Thomas Madison **had** already

become one of the few billionaires in the country.

WRONG: I had taken five courses in computer science since I came to New York University last year.

RIGHT : I **have taken** five courses in computer science since I came to New York University last year.

PRACTICE TEST

Test 1. SENTENCE COMPLETION: Choose the CORRECT answer.

1. When I got home from school, my parents_____.

   A. went to sleep

   B. had gone to sleep

2. I don't know If you _____ from University of Washington yet.

   A. had heard

   B. have heard

3. The train_____the station for Atlantic City.

   A. has just left

   B. had just left

4. By two o'clock this morning, Mary _____eighteen hours continuously with any stop.

   A. worked

   B. had worked

5. Great changes_____in the rural area since the new economic reform.

   A. had taken place

   B. have taken place

Test 2. SENTENCE CORRECTION: Choose the INCORRECT word or phrase and CORRECT it.

1. After I ~~complete~~ my studies in America, I will return to my own country.
   have completed

2. When she began her schooling, she ~~has~~ already memorized 3000 new words.
   had

3. Since I ~~am~~ grown up now, I should help my parents in finances.
   have

4. Up to now, the city ~~had~~ built five community centres.
   has

5. By the end of 1988, the number of international students in the country risen to two million.
   will have *had*

ANSWER KEY

Test 1:

1. B

2. B (Here present perfect tense should be used: *have heard*; for the action still relates to the present.)

3. A

4. B

5. B

Test 2:

1. After I **have completed** my studies in America, I will return to my own country.

2. When she began her schooling, she **had** already **memorized** 3000 new words.

3. Since I **have grown** up now, I should help my parents in finances.

4. Up to now, the city **has_built** five community centres.

5. By the end of 1988, the number of international students in the country **had risen** to two million.

LESSON 9

USE *HAVE* +PAST PARTICIPLE

WITH *SINCE, FOR,* AND

BY NOW CORRECTLY

ERROR EXAMPLE

WRONG: Monica was elected in 2010 and is the student president of our school ever since.

RIGHT: Monica was elected in 2010 and **has been** the student president of our school *ever since*.

GRAMMAR POINT

We use HAVE + Past Participle to mean that the activity is extended over a period of time. HAVE + Past Participle is especially common with adverbial expressions of duration such as *since* + time, *for* + time, and *by now*.

1. *SINCE* + TIME

The English language **has changed** greatly *since* Shakespeare's time.

Since the economic reform in 1979, dramatic changes **have taken place** in every part of China.

ERROR EXAMPLE

WRONG: The dollar had fallen more than 20 per cent since 2002.

RIGHT: The dollar **has fallen** more than 20 per cent since 2002.

In this example, the phrase *since* + time indicates that the situation still refers to the present. Therefore, the Present Perfect Tense form of the verb: *has fallen* should be used.

2. *BY NOW*

You should **have put** the milk into the refrigerator. I believe it **has become** undrinkable *by now*.

By now, several bridges **have been build** over the river.

ERROR EXAMPLE

WRONG: By now, 14 years after the last batch of prisoners was
herded naked into the gas chambers by dogs and guards, the
story of auschwitz was told a great many times.

RIGHT: *By now*, 14 years after the last batch of prisoners was
herded naked into the gas chambers by dogs and guards, the
story of Auschwitz **has been told** a great many times.

In this example, the phrase *by now* indicates that the situation still refers to
the present. Therefore, the Present Perfect Tense form of the verb: *has
been* should be used.

3. *FOR* + TIME

Michael Dickens **has waited** *for his whole life* to have a mansion

of his own. However, it turned out just to be a dream.

I **have been** away from Paris *for two weeks*.

ERROR EXAMPLE

WRONG: For thousands of years men had dreamed about fame and
fortune without any reason.

RIGHT: For thousands of years men **have dreamed** about fame and
fortune without any reason.

In this example, the phrase *for* + time indicates that the situation still refers to the present. Therefore, the Present Perfect Tense form of the verb: *have dreamed* should be used.

PRACTICE TEST

Test 1. SENTENCE COMPLETION: Choose the CORRECT answer.

1.I _____ here in New York City since 1988.

A. lived

B. have lived

2. You may by now_____ not to mix socially with economists – if you had not made that decision already.

A. have resolved

B. be resolved

3. We_____for two hours, but nobody came.

A. waited

B. have waited

4. Since the dawn of civilization, humans_____every means to conquer nature, but failed.

A. had tried

B. have tried

5. It is almost midnight, Mary should _____ to Paris by now.

A. get

B. have got

Test 2. SENTENCE CORRECTION: Choose the INCORRECT word or phrase and CORRECT it.

1. We have live in Seattle for five years.

2. He ought to arrive there by now.

3. Ray gave us a lot of help since we arrived.

4. I have took this medication since 1985.

5. We been friends since we were children.

ANSWER KEY

Test 1:

1. B

2. A

3. B

4. B

5. B

Test 2:

1. We **have lived** in Seattle *for* five years.

2. He ought to **have arrived** there *by now.*

3. Ray **has given** us a lot of help *since* we arrived.

4. I **have taken** this medication *since* 1985.

5. We **have been** friends *since* we were children.

LESSON 10

USE THE CORRECT TENSE

WITH *TIME EXPRESSIONS*

ERROR EXAMPLE

WRONG: The Senate votes on the law to ban cigarette smoking in public in 1990.

RIGHT: The Senate **voted** on the law to ban cigarette smoking in public *in* 1990.

GRAMMAR POINT

To be able to use *time expressions* correctly is fairly important; for a *time expression* clearly indicates what kind of verb tense is needed in the sentence.

Howard Jones **left** Microsoft for IBM *two years ago*.

Samuel Jackson **started** blogging for Asia Daily *last week*.

WRONG: Joy is very busy *lately*.

RIGHT: Joy **has been** very busy *lately*.

In the first example, the time expression *two years ago* indicates that the verb should be in the Simple Past Tense In the second example, the time expression *last week* indicates that the verb should be in the Simple Past Tense. In the third example, the time expression *lately* indicates that the verb should be in the Present Perfect Tense.

COMMONLY USED *TIME EXPRESSIONS*:

1.   We use the following words or phrases of time with the present perfect.

a)   *for* and **since** : We use *for* and *since* to say *how long.*

I **have been** in New York City *for twenty years.*

She **has known** George *since 1999.*

b)   **recently, in the last few days, so far:** We use *recently, in the last few days, so far* etc. indicate a period that continues until now.

I **have not seen** Bill *recently.*

She **has met** with a lot of people *in the last few days.*

George **has completed** two novels *so far* this year.

c) ***today, this morning/week/month/year***: We use *time adverbs* that refer to the present, such as *today, this morning/ week/ month/ year* etc.

We **have not received** the newspaper *today*.

The city **has built** a new stadium this *year*.

d) ***just, already, yet:*** We normally use *just, already, yet* with present perfect.

Have you **had** your dinner *yet*?

She **has** *already* **made** a lot of new friends in America since she came last month.

WRONG: We had *just* seen the new movie.

RIGHT: We **have** *just* **seen** the new movie.

2.   ***by + time (past)***: We use *by + time (past)* with Past Perfect Tense.

By 2005, many American companies **had had** business cooperation with those in the developing countries.

By ten clock this morning, we **had** already **had** two sales closed.

   WRONG: By the turn of the century, computers have become
          very popular in the developing countries.

   RIGHT: By the turn of the century, computers **had become**
             very popular in the developing countries.

PRACTICE TEST

Test 1. SENTENCE COMPLETION: Choose the CORRECT answer.

1. People's lives_____better and better ever since the country won its independence.

   A. have become

   B. had become

2. Forks and spoons_____by the people in the West for centuries.

   A. are used

   B. have been used

3. He_____to more than fifty countries in last few years.

   A. has traveled

   B. traveled

4. The little girl_____very strangely lately.

   A. had behaved

   B. has behaved

5. We_____more than twenty-five new employees so far.

   A. have recruited

   B. recruited

2. Test. SENTENCE CORRECTION: Choose the INCORRECT word or phrase and CORRECT it.

1. Have you talked to the Department Chair already?

2. Jenny had never had lobsters before.

3. He is waiting for you for a long time.

4. Since 1979 great changes took place in my hometown.

5. By 2006 our city has built more than thirty public libraries.

ANSWER KEY

Test 1:

1. A

2. B

3. A

4. B

5. A

Test 2:

1. **Have** you **talked** to the Department Chair *jet?*

2. Jenny **has** never **had** lobsters *before.*

3. He **has waited** for you *for a long time.*

4. *Since 1979* great changes **have taken** place in my hometown.

5. *By 2006* our city **had built** more than thirty public libraries.

LESSON 11

DURATION: USE *HAVE* + BEEN + PAST PARTICIPLE CORRECTLY

ERROR EXAMPLE

WRONG: Many books have written about success, but one of the best is How to Win Friends and Influence People by Dale Carnegie.

RIGHT: Many books **have been written** about success, but one of the best is How to Win Friends and Influence People by Dale Carnegie.

GRAMMAR POINT

We use HAVE + been + Past Participle to mean that a recently completed activity was extended over a period of time. Here the actor is unknown or not important and the passive form must be used.

Jenny Jones **has been accepted** to Harvard Law School.

It **has been reported** that most of the American millionaires are unhappy about their lifestyle.

In just over ten years, more than a hundred skyscrapers **have been built** in the coastal City of Dalian.

In the examples above, the completed activities do extend over a period of time and the actors are unknown. Therefore, we have to use HAVE + been + Past Participle in the passive form.

To use this structure correctly, we must avoid using HAVE + Past Participle (active form) instead of HAVE + been + Past Participle in the passive form:

WRONG: A new skytrain station has constructed in Lougheed Mall.

RIGHT: A new skytrain station **has been constructed** in Lougheed Mall.

(It is the library, not the people who built it, that is important.)

WRONG: The sick have been cured, the lost have been found, and the dead have revived.

RIGHT: The sick have been cured, the lost have been found, and the dead **have been revived**.

(It is the dead, not the people who saved them, that is important.)

PRACTICE TEST

Test 1. SENTENCE COMPLETION: Choose the CORRECT answer.

1. "We_____away by these games but we have not been intimidated," he said.

   A. have blown

   B. have been blown

2. For it might_____for more than three hundred pence, and have been given to the poor. And they murmured against her.

   A. have been sold

   B. have sold

3. Many useful compilations_____of these various chemical compounds that have been studied, and of their practical applications.

   A. has made

   B. have been made

4. Officials say four militants have been killed in the fighting so far while two troops and a special police officer have also_____.

   A. been killed

   B. killed

5. The meeting is not over until the minutes_____(within two working days) and all action items have been accomplished.

   A. have been distributed

B. have distributed

2. Test. SENTENCE CORRECTION: Choose the INCORRECT word or phrase and CORRECT it.

1. The party has planned for two weeks.

2. Your typewriter been fixed and you can pick it up any time.

3. Wayne has elected to the student government.

4. We been taught how to cook.

5. The class been changed to room 10.

ANSWER KEY

Test 1:

1. B

2. A

3. B

4. A

5. A

Test 2:

1. The party **has been planned** for two weeks.

   (*It is the party, not the people who planned it, that is important.*)

2. Your typewriter **has been fixed** and you can pick it up any time.

   (*It is your typewriter, not the people who fixed it, that is important.*)

3. Wayne **has been elected** to the student government.

   (*It is Wayne, not the people who elected him, that is important.*)

4. We **have been taught** how to cook.

   (*It is we, not the people who taught us, that is important.*)

5. The class **has been changed** to room 10.

   (*It is the class, not the people who changed it, that is important.*)

LESSON 12

PREDICTIONS: WILL

HAVE +PAST PARTICIPLE

ERROR EXAMPLE

WRONG: By year 2015, researchers will discover a cure for cancer.

RIGHT: By year 2015, researchers **will have discovered** a cure for cancer.

GRAMMAR POINT

We use Future Perfect Tense WILL *HAVE* + Past Participle and a future adverb expression to refer to a prediction for a future activity or event.

By the middle of the twenty-first century, the computer **will have become** a necessity in every home in the developing countries.

It is believed that by 2018 immunotherapy **will have succeeded** in curing a number of serious illnesses.

In the first example, the future adverb expression *by the middle of the twenty-first century* indicates that the verb should be in the Future Perfect Tense: **will have become.** In the second example, the future adverb expression *by 2018* indicates that the verb should be in the Future Perfect Tense: **will have succeeded**.

In using Future Perfect Tense to predict a future activity or event, we must avoid using WILL + Verb instead of WILL *HAVE* + Past Participle.

WRONG: I believe that I will get my doctoral degree from Harvard University by the end of 2019.

RIGHT: I believe that I **will have got** my doctoral degree from Harvard University by the end of 2019.

WRONG: They will arrive in Boston by this time tomorrow if the weather is nice.

RIGHT: They **will have arrived** in Boston by this time tomorrow if the weather is nice.

PRACTICE TEST

Test 1. SENTENCE COMPLETION: Choose the CORRECT answer.

1. Workers_____the new roads by the end of this year. By the end of next year, they will have finished work on the new stadium.

   A. will have completed

   B. will complete

2. If everything goes well, we_____fifty cars by the end of the day.

   A. have been sold

   B. will have sold

3. But American consumers_____by being denied cheap products, and China will almost certainly have retaliated

   A. will have suffered

   B. will suffer

4. The students_____their exams by six thirty.

   A. will have finished

   B. will finish

5. Indeed, the US's working age population_____by about 30 per cent, whereas China's will have dropped 3 per cent.

   A. will grow

   B. will have grown

2. Test. SENTENCE CORRECTION: Choose the INCORRECT word or phrase and CORRECT it.

1. You will finished your homework by the time the movie starts.

2. Jane will left by five o'clock.

3. Before school is out, I have returned all of my library books.

4. We will get an answer to our letter by the time we have to make a decision.

5. Before we can tell them about the discount, they will bought the tickets.

ANSWER KEY

Test 1:

1. A

2. B

3. A

4. A

5. B

Test 2:

1. You **will have finished** your homework by the time the movie starts.

2. Jane **will have left** by five o'clock.

3. Before school is out, I **will have returned** all of my library books.

4. We **will have got** an answer to our letter by the time we have to make a decision.

5. Before we can tell them about the discount, they **will have bought** the tickets.

LESSON 13

USE THE CORRECT TENSE WITH *WILL* AND *WOULD*

ERROR EXAMPLE

WRONG: He told me that he thought he will get the job in spite of his lack of education.

RIGHT: He **told** me that he thought he **would** get the job in spite of his lack of education.

GRAMMAR POINT

When we talk about something we plan to do in the future, we use the Present Future Tense: *WILL* + do something:

I **think** that I **will** leave for Los Angeles tomorrow.

Jake **doubts** that he **will** have time to finish the project.

It **is** certain that he **will** graduate from Stanford University on time.

WRONG: I know that he would arrive soon.

RIGHT: I **know** that he **will** arrive soon.

If we refer to something we planned to do in the past, we use the Past Future Tense: *WOULD* + do something:

The police officer **indicated** that he **would** write a ticket if he had the time.

The executive vice president **emphasized** at the meeting that the board **would** not change its position.

Michael **said** that he **would** come to my birthday party.

WRONG: Michael said that he will come to my birthday party.

RIGHT: Michael **said** that he **would** come to my birthday party.

In all patterns, we must avoid the error of using the combination of the past with *WILL* and present with *WOULD*.

PRACTICE TEST

Test 1. SENTENCE COMPLETION: Choose the CORRECT answer.

1. Mr. Smith said it_____be impractical to police the length of girls' skirts and said a blanket ban would be easier for staff to enforce.

   A. will

   B. would

2. Jennifer indicated that she_____take the job.

   A. would

   B. will

3. And all this beautiful silk, she_____, would be used to weave colorful clouds in heaven.

   A. says

   B. said

4. In an interview in January this year, Mr. Wang outlined a retooled strategy that he_____rejuvenate growth.

   A. says will

   B. said would

5. They promised that they_____to pay us on time.

   A. will come

   B. would come

2. Test. SENTENCE CORRECTION: Choose the INCORRECT word or phrase and CORRECT it.

1. I think I would be happy to see my brother coming back for Christmas.

2. My teacher said I will be a very good English teacher after graduation.

3. Michael agreed that he is going to help me with my mathematics.

4. The weatherman said that it will get very cold in the next few days.

5. If everything goes all right, he would come to Joyce's birthday party.

ANSWER KEY

Test 1:

1. B

2. A

3. B

4. B

5. B

Test 2:

1. I **think** I **will** be happy to see my brother coming back for Christmas.

2. My teacher **said** that I **would** be a very good English teacher after graduation.

3. Michael **agreed** that he **would** help me with my mathematics.

4. The weatherman **said** that I **would** get very cold in the next few days.

5. If everything **goes** all right, he **will** come to Joyce's birthday party.

COLUMBIA ENGLISH GRAMMAR FOR GMAT

USE THE CORRECT TENSE

AFTER *HAD HOPED*

ERROR EXAMPLE

WRONG: President Wilson had hoped that World WarIbe the last
great war, but only two decades later, the Second World
War was erupting.

RIGHT: President Wilson **had hoped** that World WarI**would be** the
last great war, but only two decades later, the Second World
War was erupting.

GRAMMAR POINT

We use *HAD HOPED* to expresses unfulfilled desires in the past or a hope that did not happen. In this pattern, *HAD HOPED* is followed by a object clause in the Past Future Tense where *WOULD* (COULD) + verb word should be used:

Although research scientists **had hoped** that the new drug interferon **would prove** to be a cure for cancer, its applications now appear to be more limited.

We **had hoped** that Mary **would change** her mind.

People **had hoped** that the government **would charge** less taxes on consumer goods.

WRONG: Hostility to nuclear power had been reversed in Sweden and many in the industry had hoped that it will be reversed in Germany as well.

RIGHT: Hostility to nuclear power had been reversed in Sweden and many in the industry had hoped that it **could** be reversed in Germany as well.

To use this pattern correctly, we must always remember that, in the object clause after *HAD HOPED*, we should never use a verb word instead of *WOULD* and a verb word.

PRACTICE TEST

Test 1. SENTENCE COMPLETION: Choose the CORRECT answer.

1. Mr. Smith said it_____be impractical to police the length of girls' skirts and said a blanket ban would be easier for staff to enforce.

   A. will

   B. would

2. Jennifer indicated that she_____take the job.

   A. would

   B. will

3. And all this beautiful silk, she_____, would be used to weave colorful clouds in heaven.

   A. says

   B. said

4. In an interview in January this year, Mr. Wang outlined a retooled strategy that he_____rejuvenate growth.

   A. says will

   B. said would

5. They promised that they_____to pay us on time.

   A. will come

   B. would come

2. Test. SENTENCE CORRECTION: Choose the INCORRECT word or phrase and CORRECT it.

1. He had hoped that he graduate this semester, but he couldn't finish his thesis in time.

2. We had hoped him staying longer.

3. They had hoped that she not find out about it.

4. I had hoped she coming to the party.

5. His father had hoped that he go into business with him.

ANSWER KEY

Test 1:

1. B

2. A

3. B

4. B

5. B

Test 2:

1. He **had hoped** that he **would graduate** this semester, but he couldn't finish his thesis in time.

2. We **had hoped** that he **would stay** longer.

3. They **had hoped** that she **would not find out** about it.

4. I **had hoped** that she **would come** to the party.

5. His father **had hoped** that he **would go** into business with him.

CHAPTER 3

NOUN CLAUSES

LESSON 15

PROBLEMS WITH
NOUN CLAUSES

ERROR EXAMPLE

WRONG: He refused to enter a plea could not be determined by the
lawyer.

RIGHT: **Why he refused to enter a plea** could not be determined
by the lawyer.

GRAMMAR POINT

In English, a noun clause is a clause that functions as a noun; because the noun clause is a noun, it is used in a sentence as either an object of a verb, an object of a preposition, or the subject of the sentence.

When the contract will be awarded is the question to be answered.

NOUN CLAUSE AS SUBJECT

He always talked with **whomever he liked**.

NOUN CLAUSE AS OBJECT

In the first example, *contract* is the subject of *will be awarded,* and the noun clause *when the contract will be awarded* is the subject of the verb *is.* In the second example, *he* is the subject of *liked*, the noun clause *whomever he liked* is the object of the preposition *with.*

Each noun clause, which has its own subject and verb, may be an embedded statement or an embedded question.

1. An embedded statement may be introduced by THAT:

That **the professor has finished grading papers** is certain.

I know *that* **he is a famous professor from the University of Rochester.**

2. An embedded question may be introduced by WH-words:

Why **the condition of that patient deteriorated so rapidly** was not explained.

Whether **or not the new office would be built** was to be determined at the meeting.

As we know, an English sentence may have more than one clause. The word that connects the clauses is called a clause connector. With regard to noun clauses, the most commonly used *noun clauses connectors* are: *what, when, where, why, how, whatever, wherever, whether, if, that.* Be careful to use them correctly with the right patterns.

A. WHAT/WHATEVER

What you have just said is absolutely right.

Whatever you do is none of my business.

B. WHEN

When you want to come to work is up to you.

I don't know **when she will leave for New York**.

C. WHY

Nobody knows **why Joyce resigned from such a high-paying job**.

Why they want to study in a foreign country is something we don't know.

D. HOW

How got accepted into Princeton University is still a mystery.

She doesn't know **how she can make a million dollars in a month**.

E. WHERE/WHEREVER

When you are down, you really don't know **where you can go**.

I will go **wherever I can find my dream job**.

F. WHETHER

I am not sure **whether I should accept this offer or not**.

Whether they will come to help us is still something unknown.

G. IF

Mary didn't know **if she had done something wrong to drive her boy friend away**.

We don't know **if he will be a good president for out country**.

H. THAT

That he is a good father is known to all in the village.

We believe **that he is the best candidate for the presidency**.

PRACTICE TEST

Test 1. SENTENCE COMPLETION: Choose the CORRECT answer.

1. Pug did not know_____was back in her good graces.

   A. he

   B. why he

2. Jack was not sure_____ should take the vacation now.

   A. if he

   B. he

3. He did not_____he had first started to talk aloud when he was by himself.

   A. remember

   B. remember when

COLUMBIA ENGLISH GRAMMAR FOR GMAT

4. Sam didn't know _____ have picked up all the right numbers for the Jackpot.

A. he got to

B. how he got to

5. I also did not know_____my environment that was harming me, or whether I was harming myself.

A. whether it was

B. it was

2. Test. SENTENCE CORRECTION: Choose the INCORRECT word or phrase and CORRECT it.

1. Thinking for many centuries that the world was flat.

2. To believe that smoking causes cancer.

3. That Mt. Everest is the highest peak in the world.

4. Do you know what time is the movie to begin?

5. Where do the aliens come from is a mystery..

ANSWER KEY

Test 1:

1. B

2. A

3. B

4. B

5. A

Test 2:

1. It was thought for many centuries **that the world was flat**.

2. It is believed **that smoking causes cancer**.

3. **That Mt. Everest is the highest peak in the world** is known to all.

4. Do you know **what time the movie is to begin**?

5. **Where the aliens come from** is a mystery.

LESSON 16

USE NOUN CLAUSE CONNECTOR/SUBJECT CORRECTLY

ERROR EXAMPLE

WRONG: There was a law in the city of Athens which gave to its citizens the power of compelling their daughters to marry whoever they pleased.

RIGHT: There was a law in the city of Athens which gave to its citizens the power of compelling their daughters to marry **whomever** they pleased.

GRAMMAR POINT

We can use NOUN CLAUSE CONNECTORS to introduce noun subject clauses. In some cases a NOUN CLAUSE CONNECTOR is not just a connector; it can also be the SUBJECT of the clause at the same time.

Whoever wants to take the desert tour during spring break must sign up at the office.

You should find out **which is the best physics department.**

We are concerned about **who will do the work.**

WRONG: We don't know whom will really come to save the poor people in today's society.

RIGHT: We don't know **who** will really come to save the poor people in today's society.

In the first example, *whoever* is the subject of the noun clause which is used as the subject of the sentence. In the second example, *which* is the subject of the noun clause which is used as the object of the sentence. In the error example, *who* is the subject of the noun clause which is used as the object of the sentence.

The following examples show how the NOUN CLAUSE CONNECTORS/SUBJECTS are used. Commonly used NOUN CLAUSE CONNECTOR/SUBJECTS are: *who, what, which, whoever, whatever, whichever*:

1. *Who* **and** *whoever* **as subject pronouns:**

Whoever comes early can claim the first prize.

Our scholarship is given to those poor students **who need** it the most.

We know **who broke** the window and **stole** our computers.

WRONG: You can give this used computer to whomever wants it.

RIGHT: You can give this used computer to **whoever** wants it.

2. *What, whatever, which, and whichever* as subject pronouns:

Who (whoever) is the suspect is totally up to the police to find out.

Children should be taught **what (whatever) is moral** early in life.

Which (whichever) is right is absolutely up to you to decide.

WRONG: Whichever interests me most are psychologies,
backgrounds and spotting winners.

RIGHT: **What interests** me most are psychologies, backgrounds
and spotting winners.

PRACTICE TEST

Test 1. SENTENCE COMPLETION: Choose the CORRECT answer.

1. _____you say about her is just your personal opinion.

A. Which

B. What

2. _____we should all learn from is really a problem in world where everyone is hunting for his own gains.

A. Who

B. Whom

3. _____is right is up to judges to decide.

A. Whom

B. Which

4. Nobody knows_____did this horrible thing to her.

A. who

B. whom

5. Stay up to date with the news to see which airports are open and _____are closed.

A. what

B. which

2. Test. SENTENCE CORRECTION: Choose the INCORRECT word or phrase and CORRECT it.

1. I will grab whatever it comes in my way.

2. Whomever has just got out of the window is unknown.

3. The committee will award the prize to whomever is the best.

4. It was hard for us to decide what was the right direction at the crossroads.

5. Dan is whom we believe can help us to design our website.

ANSWER KEY

Test 1:

1. B

2. B

3. B

4. B

5. B

Test 2:

1. I will grab **whatever comes in my way.**

2. **Whoever has just got out of the window** is unknown.

3. The committee will award the prize to **whoever is the best.**

4. It was hard for us to decide **which was the right direction at the crossroads.**

5. Dan is **who** we believe *can help us to design our website.*

LESSON 17

USE NOUN CLAUSE CONNECTOR/OBJECT CORRECTLY

ERROR EXAMPLE

WRONG: The employee was unhappy about what it was added to his job description.

RIGHT: The employee was unhappy about **what was added** to his job description.

GRAMMAR POINT

We can use NOUN CLAUSE CONNECTORS to introduce noun object clauses. In some cases a NOUN CLAUSE CONNECTOR is not just a connector; it can also be the OBJECT of the clause at the same time.

You should not buy *whatever* **your girl friend wants you to** *buy.*

I don't know *whom* **you should** *trust* **in today's world..**

WRONG: That you choose is totally up to you to decide.

RIGHT: *Whichever* **you** *choose* is totally up to you to decide.

In the first example, *whatever* is the object of the noun clause which is used as the object of the sentence. In the second example, *whom* is the object of the noun clause which is used as the object of the sentence. In the error example, *whichever* is the object of the noun clause which is used as the subject of the sentence.

The following examples show how the NOUN CLAUSE CONNECTOR/OBJECT are used. Commonly used NOUN CLAUSE CONNECTOR/OBJECTS are: *whom, whomever, what, which,, whatever, whichever*:

1. *Whom* and *whomever* as object pronouns:

You can give this book to *whom* you *like.*

People tend to blame *whomever* **they** *can find,* but never themselves for their own mistakes.

WRONG: Whoever you donate this million dollars to is absolutely

none of our business.

RIGHT: *Whomever* **you** *donate* **this million dollars** *to* is absolutely
none of our business.

2. *What, whatever, which, and whichever* as object pronouns:

You should find out *what* **you really** *want* **in life.**

Whatever **we** *do* should contribute the benefits of the people.

WRONG: The voters should elect whom of the candidates they like
best as their district representative.

RIGHT: The voters should elect *whichever* **of the candidates they**
like **best as their district representative.**

PRACTICE TEST

Test 1. SENTENCE COMPLETION: Choose the CORRECT answer.

1. This is a buffet restaurant. You can eat_____you like.

   A. whatever

   B. which

2. No one knows_____is the right direction in times of difficulty.

   A. what

   B. which

3. _____wins the competition will get a million dollars.

   A. Whomever

   B. Whoever

4. We are not sure_____is responsible for this disaster.

   A. who

   B. whom

5. I cannot say with certainty which of my motives are the strongest, but I know_____of them deserve to be followed.

   A. which

   B. whichever

2. Test. SENTENCE CORRECTION: Choose the INCORRECT word or phrase and CORRECT it.

1. You can give this used computer to who you like.

2. I know about which you did last summer.

3. W are concerned about whom will be elected as our next president.

4. Whoever you love and whatever you do will not affect my life.

5. He was a lucky person and always got whichever he wanted in life.

ANSWER KEY

Test 1:

1. A

2. B

3. B

4. A

5. A

Test 2:

1. You can give this used computer to *whomever* **you** *like.*

2. I know *what* **you** *did* **last summer**.

3. We are concerned about **who will be elected as our next president**.

4. *Whomever* **you** *love* **and whatever you do** will not affect my life.

5. He was a lucky person and always got *whatever* **he** *wanted* **in life**.

CHAPTER 4

ADJECTIVE CLAUSES

LESSON 18

PROBLEMS WITH

ADJECTIVE CLAUSES

ERROR EXAMPLE

WRONG: It could have been a simple mistake or misunderstanding,

he surely wouldn't have been discharged.

RIGHT: It could have been a simple mistake or misunderstanding,

for which he surely wouldn't have been discharged.

GRAMMAR POINT

Adjective clauses or relative clauses are a way of joining two sentences together into one sentence. In the joined sentence, the adjective clause modifies a noun or pronoun in the main clause. The adjective clause is introduced by relative pronouns (*who, whom, whose, that, which*) or relative adverbs (*when, where*). The relative pronouns and relative adverbs that introduce adjective clauses are called *clause markers*.

1. RELATIVE PRONOUNS (*who, whom, whose, that, which*) USED AS CLAUSE MARKERS:

The melting point is the temperature **at which** a solid changes to a liquid.

In life, it is not who you are but **whom** you are with.

The new BMW **which** is selling for more than a hundred thousand dollars is one of the best in the world.

The girl **whose** father is a billionaire is a Ph.D. candidate at the University of British Columbia.

WRONG: Those who live beyond the cell phone, those who have yet to see a computer, those that have no electricity at home are the ones we should care about..

RIGHT: Those who live beyond the cell phone, those who have yet to see a computer, those **who** have no electricity at home are the ones we should care about..

In the first example, relative pronoun *which* introduces the adjective clause, and *which* is used as the object of the preposition *at*. In the second example, relative pronoun *whom* introduces the adjective clause, and whom is used as the object of the preposition *with*. In the third example, relative pronoun *which* introduces the adjective clause, and *which* is used as the subject of the clause. In the fourth example, relative pronoun *whose* (possessive) introduces the adjective clause, and *whose* is used to modify *father*, the subject of the relative clause.

2. RELATIVE ADVERBS (*when, where*) USED AS CLAUSE MARKERS:

1986 is the year **when** I first visited the greatest city in the world – New York City.

This mountain village is the place **where** the President of the United States was born.

WRONG: Do not store up for yourselves treasures on earth, where moth and rust destroy, and thieves break in and steal.

RIGHT: Do not store up for yourselves treasures on earth, where moth and rust destroy, and **where** thieves break in and steal.

In the first example, relative adverb *when* introduces the adjective clause, and *when* is used as the adverb of time in the adjective clause. In the second example, relative adverb *where* introduces the adjective clause, and *where* is used as the adverb of place in the adjective clause.

PRACTICE TEST

Test 1. SENTENCE COMPLETION: Choose the CORRECT answer.

1. 1986 is the year_____I came to the united States.

   A. when

   B. that

2. Paul can still remember the village_____he first met his beautiful wife, Lisa.

   A. when

   B. where

3. Hoy is the Professor_____all the students are looking forward to meet with.

   A. whom

   B. who

4. This is the book_____will change your life forever.

   A. who

   B. which

5. The project_____Jack is responsible is going to be complete by the end of the year.

   A. which

   B. for which

2. Test. SENTENCE CORRECTION: Choose the INCORRECT word or phrase and CORRECT it.

1. He has five brothers who he loves with all his heart.

COLUMBIA ENGLISH GRAMMAR FOR GMAT

2. Shaoshan is the place that Chairman Mao was born.

3. The story that he has won the big lottery really unbelievable.

4. We established the charity foundation gave scholarships to qualified students.

5. The way how he got to Yale Law School known to nobody.

ANSWER KEY

Test 1:

1. A

2. B

3. A

4. B

5. B

Test 2:

1. He has five brothers **whom** he loves with all his heart.

2. Shaoshan is the place **where** Chairman Mao was born.

3. The story **that** he has won the big lottery is really unbelievable.

4. We established the charity foundation **which** gave scholarships to qualified students.

5. The way by **which** he got to Yale law school is known to nobody.

LESSON 19

USE ADJECTIVE CLAUSE

MARKERS CORRECTLY

ERROR EXAMPLE

WRONG: I just finished reading the novel whom the professor
suggested for my book report.

RIGHT: I just finished reading the novel **which** the professor
suggested for my book report.

GRAMMAR POINT

We use an adjective clause to modify a noun. Since the clause functions as an adjective, it is positioned directly after the noun it modifies.

The glass **that** we put on the table contains orange juice.

Harvard University is the place **where** I had the best time of my life as an aspiring young scholar.

In the first example, the relative clause introduced by the relative pronoun *that* modifies the word *glass*. In the second example, the relative clause introduced by the relative adverb *where* modifies the word *place*.

Connecting words that are used to introduce adjective clauses are called adjective *CLAUSE MARKERS*. There are two types of clause markers: one is relative pronoun such as *who, whom, whose, which,* or *that*; the other

is the relative adverb such as *when* or *where*.

1. LIST OF RELATIVE PRONOUNS USED AS CLAUSE MARKERS:

Who is used as the subject (people) of the adjective clause:

Those students **who** get an "A" on their term papers will receive a free Starbucks coupon.

A neurologist is a doctor **who** specializes in the nervous system.

Whom is used as the object (people) of the adjective clause:

National heroes are those **whom** we should all learn from.

This is the man **whom** we just saw at the subway station.

Whose is used as the possessive (people/things) of the noun (usually the subject) of the adjective clause:

Jenny is the student **whose** father is the Chairman of a large insurance company.

This is the computer genius **whose** invention changed our way of life.

Which is used as the subject/object (things) of the adjective clause:

This is the kind of books **which** interest me most.

The melting point is the temperature at **which** a solid changes to a liquid.

That is used as the subject/object (things) of the relative clause:

The famous painting **that** is on display will be auctioned for one million dollars.

The Chinese vase **that** I bought in China last year had had a history of about a thousand years.

2. LIST OF RELATIVE ADVERBS USED AS CLAUSE MAKERS:

Where is used as an adverb of place in the relative clause:

This is the little hut **where** the Nobel Prize winner was born.

A university is a place **where** great minds meet.

When is used as an adverb of time in the relative clause:

Midnight is the usual time **when** famous writers begin to write.

The year **when** the Great Depression began was the worst time in human history.

PRACTICE TEST

Test 1. SENTENCE COMPLETION: Choose the CORRECT answer.

COLUMBIA ENGLISH GRAMMAR FOR GMAT

1. He_____laughs last laughs best.

   A. who

   B. whom

2. The girl whose father is an engineer is our college flower.

   A. whose

   B. who's

3. We visited the village_____there were poor people begging for food and clothing.

   A. at which

   B. where

4. The school library_____was built last year is one of the best in the city.

   A. for which

   B. which

5. We will go_____we are needed and whenever we are needed.

   A. wherever

   B. for which

2. Test. SENTENCE CORRECTION: Choose the INCORRECT word or phrase and CORRECT it.

1. Most folk songs are ballads what use simple words and tell simple stories

2. In addition to being a naturalist, Stewart E. White was a writer his novels describe the struggle for survival on the American frontier.

3. A keystone species is a species of plants or animals its absence has a major effect on an ecological system. -

4. The movie which we watched on cable last night it was really frightening.

5. William Samuel Johnson, helped write the Constitution, became the first president of Columbia College in 1787.

ANSWER KEY

Test 1:

1. A

2. A

3. B

4. B

5. A

Test 2:

1. Most folk songs are ballads **whicch** use simple words and tell simple stories

2. In addition to being a naturalist, Stewart E. White was a writer **whose** novels describe the struggle for survival on the American frontier.

3. A keystone species is a species of plants or animals **whose** absence has a major effect on an ecological system.

4. The movie **which** we watched on cable last night **was** really frightening.

5. William Samuel Johnson, **who** helped write the Constitution, became the first president of Columbia College in 1787.

LESSON 20

INCOMPLETE ADJECTIVE CLAUSES

ERROR EXAMPLE

WRONG: There are six types of flamingos, all of them have long
legs, long necks, and beaks that curve sharply downward.

RIGHT: There are six types of flamingos, all of **which** have long
legs, long necks, and beaks that curve sharply downward.

GRAMMAR POINT

As we know, adjective clauses are a way of joining two sentences. In the
joined sentence, the adjective clause modifies a noun in another clause of

the sentence. It begins with an object CLAUSE MARKER. such as *that, which, who, whom, whose, when, and where.*

The book *that* **I wanted to borrow** had been checked out.

This is the topic *which* **interests me.**

In the first example, the two sentences **The book had been checked out** and **I wanted to borrow the book** are joined together with the adjective clause marker *that*. And *that* is used as the object of *borrow* in the adjective clause: *that I wanted to borrow.* In the second example, the two sentences **This is the topic** and **The topic interests me** are joined together with the adjective clause marker *which*. And which is used as the subject of the adjective clause: *which interests me.*

To use adjective clauses correctly, we must be very careful with the following three types of uses:

1. When the adjective clause markers *which, that,* and *whom* are used as objects in relative clauses, they can be omitted:

The new iPhone **Mary has just bought** is no better than the first edition. (*which* is omitted)

The famous Harvard professor **I wanted to see** left for Boston yesterday. (*whom* is omitted)

2. We can use adjective clause markers *which* and *whom* as objects of prepositions:

The melting point is the temperature *at* **which** a solid changes to a liquid.

These kinds of selfless heroes **whom** we should always look up *to* as our role models are very rare nowadays in our society.

3. We can also use adjective clauses in this sentence pattern: quantity word + of + adjective clause:

There were thirty-five students in our graduating class, *thirty-two of* **whom** have been accepted the top-tier national universities in the U.S.

I read a great number of books on economics, only *two of* **which** really taught me how to make my first million dollars.

PRACTICE TEST

Test 1. SENTENCE COMPLETION: Choose the CORRECT answer.

1. The international students_____are from Japan will hold Japanese-American style Christmas party on Friday.

   A. half of who

   B. half of whom

2. We shouldn't look down upon those_____come from the third world countries because of their poor economic background.

   A. that

   B. who

3. You the just the girl_____sister I want to see.

   A. whose

   B. for whose

4. The small village_____I received my college education is now a big university town.

   A. for which

   B. where

5. The women's movement_____she played a leading role came to a tragic end because of the political sanction in her country.

   A. in which

   B. for which

2. Test. SENTENCE CORRECTION: Choose the INCORRECT word or phrase and CORRECT it.

1. In geometry, a tangent is a straight line whose touching a curve at only one point.

2. It was the ragtime pianist Scott Joplin wrote the Maple Leaf Rag, perhaps the best known of all ragtime tunes.

3. Mary met with two graduate advisors, both of who she had known for years.

4. I think this is the topic which I will write my thesis.

5. Johnny Carlson is the man that everybody can count on.

ANSWER KEY

Test 1:

1. B

2. B

3. A

4. B

5. A

Test 2:

1. In geometry, a tangent is a straight line **that touches** a curve at only one point.

2. It was the ragtime pianist Scott Joplin **who** wrote the Maple Leaf Rag, perhaps the best known of all ragtime tunes.

3. Mary met with two graduate advisors, **both of whom** she had known for years.

4. I think this is the topic *on* **which** I will write my M.A. thesis.

5. Johnny Carlson is the man **whom** everybody can count on. (*whom* can also be omitted here)

CHAPTER 5

ADVERB CLAUSES

LESSON 21

INCOMPLETE

ADVERB CLAUSES

ERROR EXAMPLE

WRONG: But he also said he was more cautious about the promise of generics this time, biotech medicines were not easy to copy.

RIGHT: But he also said he was more cautious about the promise of generics this time, **because** biotech medicines were not easy to copy.

GRAMMAR POINT

An adverb clause is a subordinate clause that functions as an adverb within a main clause. It consists of a connecting word, called an adverb clause marker (subordinate conjunctions like *because, since, although, even though, while, if, unless, when, as, until, once, before, after*), and it must have a subject and a verb.

You will never known what you can accomplish in life **unless**

you try.

Even though they are tropical birds， parrots can live in temperate or even cold climates.

Great changes have taken place **since** I left my hometown twenty years ago.

In the first example, the adverb clause marker *unless* introduces an *adverb clause of condition*. In the second example, the adverb clause marker *even though* introduces an *adverb clause of concession*. In the third example, the adverb clause marker *since* introduces an *adverb clause of time*.

An adverb clause can also be introduced by adverb clause markers like *however, wherever, whenever*.

Whenever liquid magma rises to the surface of the earth, a volcano is formed.

You can put your luggage **wherever** you can find room for it.

However you solve the problem, you'll get the same answer.

In the first example, the adverb clause marker *whenever* introduces an *adverb clause of time*. In the second example, the adverb clause marker *wherever* introduces an *adverb clause of place*. In the third example, the adverb clause marker *however* introduces an *adverb clause of manner*.

PRACTICE TEST

Test 1. SENTENCE COMPLETION: Choose the CORRECT answer.

1. However, the security defaults should not be modified_____you know exactly what you are doing

   A. unless

   B. when

2. You should never give up_____there might be a lot of difficulties in your life.

   A. if

   B. even though

3. No matter whatever happens, you must try your best to succeed_____you are young.

   A. while

   B. when

4. The place_____your heart goes is the place to be.

A. where

B. that

5. If you are willing to do so, however, please feel free to take the attached sample letter and use it as a template_____you see fit.

A. for which

B. however

2. Test. SENTENCE CORRECTION: Choose the INCORRECT word or phrase and CORRECT it.

1. Despite he is good student, we can not offer him admission at this time.

2. Wherever go, you have to prove that you have enough funding for your visa.

3. Nobody can predict will happen because tomorrow is uncertain.

4. The train was late for two hours due the weather conditions in the Rockies.

5. Some students were singing when others were dancing.

ANSWER KEY

Test 1:

1. A

2. B

3. B

4. A

5. B

Test 2:

1. **Despite the fact that** he is a good student, we can not offer him admission at this time.

2. **Wherever** you go, you have to prove that you have enough funding for your visa.

3. Nobody can predict what will happen **because** tomorrow is uncertain.

4. The train was late for two hours **due to** the weather conditions in the Rockies.

5. Some students were singing **while** others were dancing.

LESSON 22

USE ADVERB *TIME* AND

CAUSE MARKERS CORRECTLY

ERROR EXAMPLE

WRONG: The family suspects a hotel employee, she said, the thieves used a copy of their electronic key to get into their room.

RIGHT: The family suspects a hotel employee, she said, **since** the thieves used a copy of their electronic key to get into their room.

GRAMMAR POINT

An adverb clause consists of a connecting word, called an adverb CLAUSE MARKER, and it must have a subject and a verb.

To use the adverb CLAUSE MARKERS correctly, we have to be careful with the following two types of adverb clauses:

1. ADVERB CLAUSE OF TIME

The common adverb *time* markers are: *after, as soon as, once, when, as, before, since, whenever, as long as, by the time, until, while.*

The children had gone to sleep **by the time** I got home last night.

You can't go anywhere **until** you finish your math homework.

We must get everything ready **before** the party begins.

You should come to see me **as soon as** you finish your project.

The plane had already taken off **when** we got Kennedy Airport.

In the examples above, the adverb clause markers *by the time, until, before, as soon as,* and *when* all introduce *adverb clauses of time.*

2. ADVERB CLAUSE OF CAUSE

The common adverb *cause* markers are: *as, now that, because, since, in as much as, in that.*

It is certain that these thing will advanced in price before long, so that we heartily advise you to buy **in as much as** you can

David did not get the job **because** he was late for the appointment,.

Now that you have got your degree, it is time for you to find a job.

You might as well stay at home **since** there is nothing to do in the office.

Mercury differs from other industrial metals **in that** it is a liquid.

In the examples above, the adverb clause markers *in as much as, because, now that, since,* and *in that* all introduce *adverb clauses of cause.*

PRACTICE TEST

Test 1. SENTENCE COMPLETION: Choose the CORRECT answer.

1. _____ it is very hard to score high on the test, we must try our best to prepare for the best.

   A. Despite

   B. Since

2. We promise that we will not go home_____we finish our job.

   A. when

B. until

3. _____the debtor has no property, I abandoned the claim.

   A. In as much as

   B, when

4. You can call us_____you need any assistance with your homework or term papers.

   A. whenever

   B. as

5. Sylvia Browne is an exception_____she's the only professional psychic in the whole world that has accepted our challenge.

   A. in that

   B. that

2. Test. SENTENCE CORRECTION: Choose the INCORRECT word or phrase and CORRECT it.

1. Tom didn't practice driving, and he failed his road test..

2. They got to the railway station and the train had already left.

3. The graduation party didn't begin as all the students arrive.

4. I have made quite a few friends when I cam to New York City.

5. Maple wrote our new business plan while I did the local market research..

ANSWER KEY

Test 1:

1. B

2. B

3. A

4. A

5. A

Test 2:

1. **Because** Tom didn't practice driving, he failed his road test.

2. **By the time** they got to the railway station, the train had already left.

3. The graduation party did not begin **until** all the students arrive.

4. I have made quite a few friends **since** I cam to New York City.

5. Maple wrote our new business plan, **and** I did the local market research.

LESSON 23

USE ADVERB *CONTRAST,* *CONDITION, MANNER,* AND *PLACE* MARKERS CORRECTLY

ERROR EXAMPLE

WRONG: Chanel could run miles in her younger days, now she suffers from joint problems and spends most of her days at home.

RIGHT: **Although** Chanel could run miles in her younger days, now she suffers from joint problems and spends most of her days at home.

GRAMMAR POINT

An adverb clause consists of a connecting word, called an adverb CLAUSE MARKER, and it must have a subject and a verb.

To use adverb CLASUE MARKERS correctly, we have to pay special attention to the following types of adverb clauses:

1. ADVERB CLAUSE OF CONTRAST

The common adverb *contrast* markers are: *although, even though, though, while,* and *whereas*

Even though Mr. Nicolson is not very rich, he is always willing to help those in need.

The rich are getting richer and richer **while** the poor are getting poorer and poorer in today's world.

WRONG: We thought she didn't like us, in fact she was very shy.

RIGHT:　We thought she didn't like us, **whereas** in fact she was very shy.

2. ADVERB CLAUSE OF CONDITION

The common adverb *condition* markers are: *if, in case, provided, providing, unless,* and *whether.*

If the automobile had not been invented, what would people use for basic transportation?

You will go to Beijing with us for the summer **provided** you pass the state test.

You will never succeed **unless** you try.

WRONG: I will lend you my cell phone but you return it to me in a week.

RIGHT: I will lend you my cell phone **providing** you return it to me in a week.

3. ADVERB CLAUSE OF MANNER

The adverb *manner* markers are: *as, as if,* and *as though.*

When in Rome, do **as** the Romans do.

He looks **as if** he is a multimillionaire.

WRONG: She cried so sadly like the sky was falling down.

RIGHT: She cried so sadly **as though** the sky was falling down.

4. ADVERB CLAUSE OF PLACE

The adverb *place* markers are: *where, wherever.*

Wherever he goes, there is always trouble.

When you have nowhere to go, you might as well stay **where** you are.

WRONG: With today's communication tools, you can go to wherever you like to go in a day.

RIGHT: With today's communication tools, you can go **wherever** you like to go in a day.

PRACTICE TEST

Test 1. SENTENCE COMPLETION: Choose the CORRECT answer.

1. The old woman was moved to ears just_____she has won the lottery.

   A. for

   B. as if

2. Mary is very modest_____she is the best student in our class,

   A. and

   B. although

3. You can not go to the movie with Jack_____you finish your homework on time.

   A. except for

   B. unless

4. I will not offer any more help to you_____you get straight A's in all your courses next semester.

A. provided

B. as

5. Make sure they are all sealed tightly, and keep them in a plastic case of bag_____they leak.

A. where

B. in case

2. Test. SENTENCE CORRECTION: Choose the INCORRECT word or phrase and CORRECT it.

1. A good time is where time goes by quickly.

2. I will go with you unless you drive.

3. As you want less noise, you can move to the country.

4. President Kennedy committed the U.S. to being the first to land on the moon, and he died before he saw his dream realized.

5. This secret cove is rumoured to be the place that the first emperor of China was buried.

ANSWER KEY

Test 1:

1. B

2. B

3. B

4. A

5. B

Test 2:

1. A good time is **when** time goes by quickly.

2. I will go with you **provided that** you drive.

3. **If** you want less noise, you can move to the country.

4. President Kennedy committed the U.S. to being the first to land on the moon, **but** he died before he saw his dream realized.

5. This secret cove is rumoured to be the place **where** the first emperor of China was buried.

LESSON **24**

USE ADVERB *CAUSE-AND-RESULT* MARKERS CORRECTLY

ERROR EXAMPLE

WRONG: Albert Einstein was such brilliant a scientist that many of his colleagues had to study for several years in order to form opinions about his theories.

RIGHT: Albert Einstein was **such a** brilliant scientist that many of his colleagues had to study for several years in order to form opinions about his theories.

GRAMMAR POINT

In an ADVERB CLAUSE OF RESULT introduced by the adverb clause markers *such...that* and *so...that*, the *such/so* clause expresses *CAUSE* and the *that* clause expresses *RESULT*. In each clause, there must be a subject and a verb.

1. ADVERB CLAUSE MARKER: *SUCH...THAT*:

Remember that such is used before an count noun or noncount noun followed by *that*. The *such* clause expresses *cause* and the *that* clause expresses *result*.

Water is **such an** excellent solvent **that** it generally contains dissolved materials in greater or lesser amounts.

This is **such** good news **that** I will call my wife right away.

WRONG: Jenny is such nice girl that everybody loves her.

RIGHT: Jenny is **such a** nice girl **that** everybody loves her.

In the first example, *such* modifies a count noun *solvent*, therefore, an indefinite article *an* is used to modify *excellent solvent*. In the second example, *such* modifies a noncount noun *news*, therefore, no article is need. In the error example, *such* modifies a count noun *girl*, therefore, an indefinite article *a* is used to modify *nice girl*.

2. ADVERB CLAUSE MARKER: *SO...THAT*:

Remember that *so* is used before an adjective or an adverb followed by *that*. The *so* clause expresses *cause* and the *that* clause expresses *result*.

The music was **so** loud **that** we could hardly hear anything.

We got to the airport **so** late **that** we missed our flight to New York.

By the mid-nineteenth century, land was **so** expensive in large cities **that** architects began to conserve space by designing skyscrapers

WRONG: By the mid-nineteenth century, land was very expensive in large cities that architects began to conserve space by designing skyscrapers.

RIGHT: By the mid-nineteenth century, land was **so** expensive in large cities **that** architects began to conserve space by designing skyscrapers.

In the first example, *so* modifies the word *loud*, which is used as an adjective. In the second example, *so* modifies the word *late*, which is used here as an adverb. In the error example, we should use *so* to modify the word *expensive*, which is used here as an adjective.

PRACTICE TEST

Test 1. SENTENCE COMPLETION: Choose the CORRECT answer.

1. Vancouver is_____ nice city that it attracts the most immigrant investors in Canada.

   A. such a

152

B. so

2. Jenny is so beautiful_____all the boys like to go out with her.

A. so that

B. that

3. It was_____early that I could hardly get up.

A. such an

B. so

4. Jack is_____nice young man that everybody in the village loves him.

A. such

B. such a

5. The homeless girl drank_____beer that she could hardly stand up.

A. much

B. so much

2. Test. SENTENCE CORRECTION: Choose the INCORRECT word or phrase and CORRECT it.

1. It was so interesting book that he couldn't put it down.

2. She is such nice girl that everyone likes her..

3. We arrived so late as Professor Baker had already called the roll.

4. Preparing frozen foods is too easy that anyone can do it.

5. It is so nice weather that I would like to go to the beach.

ANSWER KEY

Test 1:

1. A

2. B

3. B

4. B

5. B

Test 2:

1. It was **such an** interesting book **that** he couldn't put it down.

(or It was **so** interesting **a** book **that** he couldn't put it down.)

2. She is **such a** nice girl **that** everyone likes her..

(or She is **so** nice **a** girl **that** everyone likes her.)

3. We arrived **so late that** Professor Baker had already called the roll.

4. Preparing frozen foods is **so easy that** anyone can do it.

5. It is **such** nice weather **that** I would like to go to the beach.

CHAPTER 6

PARALLEL STRUCTURES

LESSON 25

USE PARALLEL STRUCTURE WITH COORDINATE CONJUNCTIONS CORRECTLY

ERROR EXAMPLE

WRONG: Jimmy likes to go crab fishing during the day, but Justin prefers catching sharks at night.

RIGHT: Jimmy likes **to go** crab fishing during the day, but Justin prefers **to catch** sharks at night.

GRAMMAR POINT

We use coordinate conjunctions (*and, but, or yet, for, nor*) to join together equal expressions. These conjunctions can join nouns, verbs, adjectives, phrases, subordinate clauses, and main clauses. To use them correctly, we must make sure that what is on one side of these coordinate conjunctions must be parallel to what is on the other side. In other words, we must join together two of the same thing.

> We will not give up **nor** will we make any compromise with our goal of being the best computer company in the world.
>
> He is both intelligent **and** courageous.
>
> She was glad to go home, and **yet** most woefully sad to leave school.
>
> WRONG: Peter Johnson is not a professor nor is he a lawyer.
>
> RIGHT: Peter Johnson is not a professor **nor** a lawyer.
>
> WRONG: I am not interested in what you are saying about it but your doing it.
>
> RIGHT: I am not interested in what you are saying about it **but**
>
>   how you are doing it.
>
> WRONG: Jennifer likes hiking and to go fishing.
>
> RIGHT: Jennifer likes hiking **and** fishing.

In the first error example, two nouns *professor* and *lawyer* are joined together by the coordinate conjunction *nor*. In the second error example, two clauses *what you are saying about it* and *how you are doing it* are joined together by the coordinate conjunction *but*. In the third error example, two gerunds *hiking* and *fishing* are joined together by the coordinate conjunction *and*.

The following examples show you how the common types of parallel structures are formed by coordinate conjunctions.

1. TWO VERBS JOINED BY COORDINATE CONJUNCTIONS.

David ate **and** slept in the lab when he was writing his research paper.

You can talk to her **but** never go out with her.

We can go to the movie **or** play cards at home.

2. TWO ADJECTIVES JOINED BY COORDINATE CONJUNCTIONS.

This girl is truly beautiful **and** smart.

The president's speech was long **but** interesting.

Man can be good **or** bad. It's all up to you to make the judgment.

3. TWO PHRASES JOINED BY COORDINATE CONJUNCTIONS.

In the spring, there are flowers in front of my house **and** in my backyard.

The books are on my desk **or** on the floor.

You will get your checks not in the morning **but** in the afternoon.

4. TWO CLAUSES JOINED BY COORDINATE CONJUNCTIONS.

I am not worried about what you do *or* how you will survive.

We are here because we don't want to miss the movie **and** because my daughter is the leading actress.

Scot wants to go to Paris for his vacation, **but** his parents want to go to the countryside for their summer holidays.

PRACTICE TEST

Test 1. SENTENCE COMPLETION: Choose the CORRECT answer.

1. It is, therefore, imperative that it be shielded from regional and national influence and not_____.

   A. be captured by particular interests

   B. captured by particular interests

2. Nancy suggested taking the plane this evening or _____.

   A. going by train tomorrow

   B. that we go by train tomorrow

3. We are not worried about what you do_____how you are going to take care of your people.

   A. and

   B. but

4. The enemy strapped him,and_____he said nothing.

A. yet

B. but

5. A smile costs nothing, _____gives much.

A. and

B. but

Test 2. SENTENCE CORRECTION: Choose the INCORRECT word or phrase and CORRECT it.

1. Jennifer thought it was essential that she succeed and skiing.

2. He love her dearly but not her cat.

3. Jake left his pet rabbit out in the cold and alone.

4. I wanted to go to the party, and Peter never intended to go.

5. Christine worked very hard, and she knew she would not keep her job if she did not.

ANSWER KEY

Test 1:

1. A (**it   be captured**: use the same kind of passive voice like *it be shielded*)

2. A (**taking   going**...are of the same thing: *gerunds*.)

3. B

4. A

5. B

Test 2:

1. Jennifer thought it was essential that **she succeed *and* that she ski** regularly.

2. He **loved her** dearly *but* he **did not love her cat**.

3. Jake left his pet rabbit **out in the cold *and* by itself**.

4. I wanted to go to the party, **yet** Peter never intended to go.

5. Christine worked very hard, **for** she knew she would not keep her job if she did not.

LESSON 26

USE PARALLEL STRUCTURE WITH CORRELATIVE CONJUNCTIONS CORRECTLY

ERROR EXAMPLE

WRONG: Reservation of a necessary portion of an estate shall be made in a will for a successor who neither can work or he has a source of income.

RIGHT: Reservation of a necessary portion of an estate shall be made in a will for a successor who **neither** can work **nor** has a source of income.

GRAMMAR POINT

The paired correlative conjunctions *both... and, either... or, neither... nor,* and *not only... but also, whether...or* to join together equal expressions or form parallel structures. And they must join together two of the same thing.

He is **both** intelligent **and** trustworthy.

This man is either a teacher or an engineer.

When we were poor, we had **neither** food **nor** clothing.

Whether you like it **or** not does not affect my decision to go to study

in the United States.

WRONG: He is not only an excellent student but also he is an

outstanding athlete.

RIGHT: He is **not only** an excellent student **but also** an

outstanding athlete.

WRONG: Mary is neither pretty or charming.

RIGHT: Mary is **neither** pretty **nor** charming

WRONG: The tickets are in my purse or in my pocket.

RIGHT: The tickets are **either** in my purse **or** in my pocket.

In the first error example, the paired correlative conjunction *not only...but also...* join two equal nouns: *student* and *athlete*. In the second error example, the paired correlative conjunction *neither...nor...*join two equal adjectives: *pretty* and *charming*. In the third error example, the paired correlative conjunction *either...or...*join two equal prepositional phrases: *in my purse* and *in my pocket*.

The following examples show you how the common types of parallel structures are formed by correlative conjunctions.

1. TWO NOUNS JOINED BY CORRELATIVE CONJUNCTIONS.

Professor MacDonald speaks **neither** French **nor** German.

She is **either** a writer **or** a professor.

2. TWO INFINITIVES JOINED BY CORRELATIVE CONJUNCTIONS.

He wants **either** to go by train **or** to go by plane.

The instructor intends **neither** to please the students **nor** to punish them.

3. TWO ADJECTIVES JOINED BY CORRELATIVE CONJUNCTIONS.

The City of Vancouver is **not only** beautiful **but also** friendly.

This book is **both** well-written **and** professionally designed.

4. TWO PHRASES JOINED BY CORRELATIVE CONJUNCTIONS.

You luggage is **neither** in the airport **nor** on another plane.

I think I have left my wallet **either** in my car **or** in my office.

5. TWO CLAUSES JOINED BY CORRELATIVE CONJUNCTIONS.

To this day, it's unclear **whether** he shot himself **or** he was murdered.

We know **both** where he will stay **and** what he will do in New York.

PRACTICE TEST

Test 1. SENTENCE COMPLETION: Choose the CORRECT answer.

1. It was not clear from the statement if either remained at their estate

in Brentwood, _____.

A. or whom the children were with.

B. and whom the children were with.

2. The new movie was neither amusing nor_____.

A. was it interesting.

B. interesting

3. They are neither interested in our products_____they willing to do any business with us.

A. nor are

B. or are

4. Either he_____his friends are they people we can trust.

A. nor

B. or

5. They have decided not only to help us with the research project_____to provide support for our finances.

A. but also

B. but

Test 2. SENTENCE CORRECTION: Choose the INCORRECT word or phrase and CORRECT it.

1. He is neither well qualified or sufficiently experienced for that position.

2. That horse is not only the youngest one in the race and the only one to win two years in a row.

3. Neither the public or the private sector of the economy will be seriously affected by this regulation.

4. He refused to work either in Chicago nor in Vancouver.

5. Mary decided not only to start a diet, but to join a fitness club.

ANSWER KEY

Test 1:

1. A (**either   or**)

2. B (**neither amusing...nor interesting**...are of the same thing: *adjectives*)

3. A

4. B

5. A

Test 2:

1. He is **neither** well qualified **nor** sufficiently experienced for that position.

2. That horse is **not only** the youngest one in the race **but also** the only one to win two years in a row.

3. **Neither** the public **nor** the private sector of the economy will be seriously affected by this regulation.

4. He refused to work **either** in Chicago **or** in Vancouver.

5. Mary decided **not only** to start a diet, **but also** to join a fitness club.

LESSON 27

USE PARALLEL STRUCTURE
WITH COMPARISONS CORRECTLY

ERROR EXAMPLE

WRONG: The collection of foreign journals in the university library is more extensive than the high school library.

RIGHT: The **collection** of foreign journals in the university library is *more* extensive *than* **the one** in the high school library.

GRAMMAR POINT

In making a comparison, we point out the similarities or differences between two things, and those similarities or differences must be in parallel form.

1. We can recognize a comparison showing how two things are different from the *–er… than , more… than* **or** *less…than.*

His research for the thesis was *more* useful *than* hers.

Dining in the restaurant is *more* fun *than* eating at home.

This lesson is *more* difficult *than* the one we had before.

WRONG: You have fewer homework than they do.

RIGHT: You have *less* homework *than* they do.

2. We can recognize a comparison showing how two things are the same from the expressions such as *as… as …, the same as…, similar to…or like.*

A. *AS…AS…*

Bill is *as* smart *as* Michael.

Leone is *as* pretty *as* her Jessica.

B. *THE SAME AS…LIKE*

Mary is *the same* height *as* Bill.

Tom is *the same* age *as* Peter.

C. LIKE, THE SAME AS

Your car is *like* mine.

Your car is *the same as* mine.

D. *SIMILAR TO*

My iPhone is *similar to* yours.

The economic situation here is very much *similar to* that in Asia.

WRONG: The IP address is not the same like the IP address of the Windows cluster, but it must be in the same subnet as the Windows cluster.

RIGHT: The IP address is not **the same as** the IP address of the Windows cluster, but it must be in the same subnet as the Windows cluster.

PRACTICE TEST

Test 1. SENTENCE COMPLETION: Choose the CORRECT answer.

1. Our classroom is_____than your seminar room.

   A. much bigger

   B. more bigger

2. Vancouver is more beautiful than_____.

   A. any city in North America

   B. any other city in North America

3. We have_____natural resources than any other country in the world.

   A. more

   B. the most

4. Your laptop is just_____mine.

   A. like

   B. the same like

5. Favorable weather is_____than advantageous terrain, and advantageous terrain is less important than unity among the people.

   A. least important

   B. less important

Test 2. SENTENCE CORRECTION: Choose the INCORRECT word or phrase and CORRECT it.

1. Joyce is more smarter than her classmates.

2. This building is more expensive as that one.

3. John's salary was much larger than Tom.

4. The number of college students this year is larger than last year.

5. Susan is more clever than anybody in her class.

ANSWER KEY

Test 1:

1. A

2. B

3. A

4. A

5. B

Test 2:

1. Joyce is **smarter *than*** her classmates.

2. This building is ***more*** expensive ***than*** that one.

3. John's salary was much larger ***than* Tom's**

4. The number of college students this year is larger *than* **that of** last year.

5. Susan is *more* clever *than* **any other student** in her class.

CHAPTER 7

CONDITIONAL SENTENCES AND WISHES

LESSON 28

USE CONDITIONALS:

IMPOSSIBLE SITUATION IN

PRESENT TIME CORRECTLY

ERROR EXAMPLE

WRONG: If Americans ate fewer foods with sugar and salt, their general health will be better.

RIGHT: .If Americans **ate** fewer foods with sugar and salt, their general health **would** be better.

GRAMMAR POINT

When we use conditionals which refer to the impossible or unreal situations in present time, we use the Past Tense in the *if*-clause and *would, could,* or *might,* + the simple verb in the result clause. The meaning is present, not past.

If weather **were** nice, we **would go** fishing.

If I **had** million dollars, I **would build** school for the poor.

If she **had** a doctoral degree, she **might consider** teaching in a college.

If you **had** a brother, you **could count on** him for help in times of difficulties.

If she **were** a bird, she **would fly** in the sky.

WRONG: If we found her luggage, we will call her.

RIGHT: .If we **found** her luggage, we **would call** her.

WRONG: If drivers obeyed the speed limit, fewer accidents occur.

RIGHT: .If drivers **obeyed** the speed limit, fewer accidents **would occur**.

WRONG: If I were a bird, I shall fly to New York City for a visit.

RIGHT: .If I **were** a bird, I **would fly** to New York City for a visit.

WRONG: If my sister was here, I would not feel so lonely in a foreign country.

RIGHT: .If my sister **were** here, I **would not feel** so lonely in a foreign country.

WRONG: If Michael had a million dollars, he will spend it in a week.

RIGHT: .If Michael **had** a million dollars, he **would spend** it in a week.

PRACTICE TEST

Test 1. SENTENCE COMPLETION: Choose the CORRECT answer.

1. If it_____fine, we would go out and play.

   A. was

   B. were

2. If he_____only a few good friends, he would not feel that lonely.

   A. had

   B. has

3. If his parents had enough money, Michael_____need to apply for a student loan.

A. will not

B. would not

4. If she_____still young, she would go to Hollywood.

A. is

B. were

5. If I had the opportunity to meet the president of the company, I_____definitely give my proposal to him in person.

A. would

B. will

Test 2. SENTENCE CORRECTION: Choose the INCORRECT word or phrase and CORRECT it.

1. If Jim's family meet Karen, I am sure that they would like her.

2. If you made your bed in the morning, your room looks better when you got back in the afternoon.

3. If Judy didn't drink so much coffee, she wouldn't have been so nervous

4. If you would go to bed earlier, you wouldn't be so sleepy in the morning.

5. If she would eat fewer sweets, she would lose weight.

ANSWER KEY

Test 1:

1. B

2. A

3. B

4. B

5. A

Test 2:

1. *If* **Jim's family met** Karen, I am sure that **they would like** her.

   or

   I am sure that **they would like** her *if* **Jim's family met** Karen.

2. *If* **you made** your bed in the morning, **your room would look** better when you got back in the afternoon.

   or

   Your room would look better when you got back in the afternoon *if* **you made** your bed in the morning.

3. *If* **Judy didn't drink** so much coffee, **she wouldn't be** so nervous.

   or

   Judy wouldn't be so nervous *if* **she didn't drink** so much coffee.

4. *If* **you went** to bed earlier, **you wouldn't be** so sleepy in the morning.

or

You wouldn't be so sleepy in the morning **if you went** to bed earlier.

5. *If* **she ate** fewer sweets, **she would lose** weight.

or

She **would lose** weight **if she ate** fewer sweets.

LESSON 29

USE CONDITIONALS:

IMPOSSIBLE SITUATION

IN PAST TIME CORRECTLY

ERROR EXAMPLE

WRONG: According to some historians, if Napoleon had not invaded Russia, he would conquer the rest of Europe.

RIGHT: . According to some historians, if Napoleon **had not invaded** Russia, he **would have conquered** the rest of Europe.

GRAMMAR POINT

When we use conditionals which refer to the impossible or unreal situations in past time, we use the Past Perfect Tense in the *if*-clause and *would*, *could*, or *might* + *have* + the past participle in the result clause. The meaning is past, not present.

If he **had had** a billion dollars, he **would have donated** it all to the

United Way then.

If I **had been** a computer scientist, I **would have started** my own

software company.

Had I **met** you at Harvard University, I **would have married** you.

WRONG: If I had found her address, I would write her.

RIGHT: .If I **had found** her address, I **would have written** her.

WRONG: If she had the opportunity to go to Wall Street, she would
have become a billionaire at age twenty-five.

RIGHT: .If she **had had** the opportunity to go to Wall Street, she
would have become a billionaire at age twenty-five.

WRONG: If Thomas had listened to his wife, he wouldn't become
homeless.

RIGHT: .If Thomas **had listened** to his wife, he **wouldn't have
become** homeless.

WRONG: If Marilyn were married to me, she would have become the happiest woman on earth.

RIGHT: .If Marilyn **had been married** to me, she **would have become** the happiest woman on earth.

WRONG: If dinosaurs would have continued roaming the earth, man would have evolved quite differently.

RIGHT: .If dinosaurs **had continued** roaming the earth, man **would have evolved** quite differently.

PRACTICE TEST

Test 1. SENTENCE COMPLETION: Choose the CORRECT answer.

1. If he had studied harder, he_____the exam.

   A. would not have failed

   B. would not fail

2. If she _____enough money, she would definitely help you.

   A. has

   B. had

3. If I had published my bestseller when I was young,
   I_____a millionaire.

   A. would have become

B. would become

4. If I_____the scholarship to go to Columbia University, I would have got my Ph.D. in economics.

   A. had

   B. had had

5. If you had treated them fairly, they_____you without even a notice.

    A. wouldn't have left

    B. wouldn't leave

Test 2. SENTENCE CORRECTION: Choose the INCORRECT word or phrase and CORRECT it.

1. If we had the money, we would have bought a new stereo system.

2. If the neighbors hadn't quieted down, I would have to call the police.

3. If her mother let her, Anne would have stayed longer.

4. If we would have known that she had planned to arrive today, we could have met her at the bus station.

5. If I had more time, I would have checked my paper again.

ANSWER KEY

Test 1:

1. A

2. B

3. A

4. B

5. A

Test 2:

1. *If* **we had had** the money, **we would have bought** a new stereo system.

or

We would have bought a new stereo system *if* **we had had** the money.

2. *If* **the neighbors hadn't quieted down, I would have had** to call the police.

or

I would have had to call the police *if* **the neighbors hadn't quieted down.**

3. *If* **her mother had let** her, **Anne would have stayed** longer.

or

Anne would have stayed longer *if* **her mother had let** her.

4. *If* we had known that she had planned to arrive today, we could have met her at the bus station.

or

We could have met her at the bus station *if* we had known that she had planned to arrive today.

5. *If* I had had more time, I would have checked my paper again.

or

I would have checked my paper again *if* I had had more time.

LESSON 30

INVERT THE SUBJECT AND

VERB WITH CONDITIONALS

ERROR EXAMPLE

WRONG: When a lovely woman says you look like her fiancé, it

means was she not engaged, you'd be able to win her love.

RIGHT: .When a lovely woman says you look like her fiancé, it

means **were** she not engaged, you'd be able to win her
love.

GRAMMAR POINT

The inversion of the subject and verb in conditional structures occurs when the helping verb in the conditional clause is *had, should*, or *were*, and the conditional connector *if* is omitted.

Were I fresh eighteen, I would marry the Prince of Wales.

Had I **had** a billion dollars, I would have built a mansion like that of

Bill Gates.

Should I **meet** her again, I would tell her the truth.

WRONG: Had Mary Lincoln know how much pernicious mischief
            Herndon would perpetrate in later years, she would have
            been more self-serving.

RIGHT: .**Had** Mary Lincoln **known** how much pernicious mischief
            Herndon would perpetrate in later years, she would have
            been more self-serving.

WRONG: I would definitely help you was I in a position to help.

RIGHT: .I would definitely help you **were** I in a position to help.

PRACTICE TEST

Test 1. SENTENCE COMPLETION: Choose the CORRECT answer.

1. Had you studied harder, your test score should be higher.

   A. would have been higher

   B. should be higher

2. Had it not been for your invaluable assistance with my application, _____.

   A. I would not have been accepted by Harvard Law School

   B. I would not be accepted by Harvard Law School

3. _____I meet him in the library again, I would give this dictionary to him.

   A. Had

   B. Should

4. I would have found my dream job in the Silicon Valley_____I had a computer degree from Stanford.

   A. had

   B. should

5. _____she my mother, I would feel very proud of her.

   A. Were

   B. Was

Test 2. SENTENCE CORRECTION: Choose the INCORRECT word or phrase and CORRECT it.

1. Was she there, she would make a speech at the university.

2. Has there been a chance, I would have taken it.

3. Lost your job, what would you have done?

4. Had they asked me, I would give my opinion yesterday.

5. Had Bob study more, he would have passed the test.

ANSWER KEY

Test 1:

1. A (Here past future perfect tense *would have been* should be used because in the inverted adverbial clause of condition, past perfect tense *had...studied* is used.)

2. A (In the conditional clause, we used past perfect tense, therefore, in the main clause, we should use past future perfect tense: *would not have been accepted.*)

3. B

4. A

5. A

Test 2:

1. **Were** she there, she would make a speech at the university.

2. **Had** there **been** a chance, I would have taken it.

3. **Had** you **lost** your job, what would you have done?

4. Had they asked me, I **would have given** my opinion yesterday.

5. **Had** Bob **studied** more, he would have passed the test.

LESSON 31

USE NOUNS DERIVED FROM CONDITIONAL VERBS CORRECTLY

ERROR EXAMPLE

WRONG: Council agrees in general to the recommendation that the condition for the dependant to live with the applicant is relaxed.

RIGHT: .Council agrees in general to the recommendation that the condition for the dependant to live with the applicant **be relaxed.**

GRAMMAR POINT

Remember that the following nouns derived from conditional verbs are most often used in this pattern:

demand, insistence, preference, proposal, recommendation, request requirement, suggestion:

He said he shortchanges his lecture on the accords because of North Carolina's **recommendation** that he also **cover** the airlines.

Our **requirement** is that everybody **be** here at 6:30am sharp.

He didn't dispute one senator's **suggestion** that the pause **be** several months long.

His **request** that the matter **be looked into** again was rudely refused by the police.

WRONG: Mary Jones thought the editor's insistence that she makes clear that the story was a spoof was unnecessary.

RIGHT: .Mary Jones thought the editor's **insistence** that she **make** clear that the story was a spoof was unnecessary.

WRONG: But in order not to weary you further, I would insist on my request that you are kind enough to hear us briefly.

RIGHT: .But in order not to weary you further, I would insist on my **request** that you **be** kind enough to hear us briefly.

WRONG: The recommendation that school teachers are evaluated for stipend every year was approved.

RIGHT: .The **recommendation** that school teachers **be evaluated** for stipend every year was approved.

PRACTICE TEST

Test 1. SENTENCE COMPLETION: Choose the CORRECT answer.

1. The proposal that our downtown college bookstore_____on Sundays was welcomed.

   A. stays open

   B. stay open

2. Everybody liked my suggestion that Gordon McDonald _____.

   A. is running for the next President of the United States

   B. run for the next President of the United States

3. Mary's proposal that we_____a vacation in Paris was approved by the president of the company.

   A. take

   B. must take

4. Jack's request that his application_____was denied by the school.

A. is reconsidered

B. be reconsidered

5. This is my demand that overdue rent_____within the next forty-eight hours.

A. must be paid

B. be paid

Test 2. SENTENCE CORRECTION: Choose the INCORRECT word or phrase and CORRECT it.

1. He complied with the requirement that all graduate students in education should write a thesis.

2. The committee refused the request that the prerequisite shall be waived.

3. She ignored the suggestion that she gets more exercise.

4. The terrorist's demand that the airline provides a plane will not be met by the deadline.

5. He regretted not having followed his advisor's recommendation that he dropping the class.

ANSWER KEY

Test 1:

1. B (Here the simple form of the verb *stay* should be used after the noun *proposal* derived from subjunctive verb *propose*.)

2. B (Here the simple form of the verb *run* must be used even if it is in the third person singular.)

3. A

4. B

5. B

Test 2:

1. He complied with the **requirement** that all graduate students in education **write** a thesis.

2. The committee refused the **request** that the prerequisite **be waived**.

3. She ignored the **suggestion** that she **get** more exercise.

4. The terrorist's **demand** that the airline **provide** a plane will not be met by the deadline.

5. He regretted not having followed his advisor's **recommendation** that he **drop** the class.

LESSON 32

USE PRESENT WISHES AND PAST WISHES CORRECTLY

ERROR EXAMPLE

WRONG: I wish there are no hunger and poverty in this world.

RIGHT: . I **wish** there **were** no hunger and poverty in this world.

GRAMMAR POINT

When we express present wishes which refer to the impossible or unreal situations in present time, we use the Past Tense in the *wish*-clause.

Joyce **wishes** that she **were** still in her fresh sixteen.

I **wish** that I **lived** in a huge mansion by the sea.

We always **wish** that we **had** billion dollars in the bank.

Tom **wishes** that he **opened** his own restaurant.

WRONG: Paul wishes that he has a billion dollars in his bank account.

RIGHT: . Paul **wishes** that he **had** a billion dollars in his bank account.

WRONG: I wish that I live in Los Angeles.

RIGHT: . I **wish** that I **lived** in Los Angeles.

WRONG: Mary wishes that she was still in her fresh eighteen.

RIGHT: . Mary **wishes** that she **were** still in her fresh eighteen.

Remember that always use *were* in present wishes for linking verb *to be* no matter whether it is the first person, second person or third person singular or plural.

Jack's mother has always **wished** that she **were** still the

college flower.

She often **wishes** that she were the daughter of a billionaire.

They often **wish** that they were not toiling like pigs on a farm.

When we express past wishes which refer to the impossible or unreal situations in past time, we use the Past Perfect Tense in the *wish*-clause.

They **wish** that they **had not started** that company.

She **wishes** that her husband **had given** her more money

for cosmetics.

We **wish** that we **hadn't wasted** too much time having fun at college.

WRONG: Sammy wishes that he passed the TOEFL test before

coming to the United States.

RIGHT: . Sammy **wishes** that he **had passed** the TOEFL test before

coming to the United States.

WRONG: Jason and Jenny wish that they received fellowships before
they got to Stanford University.

RIGHT: . Jason and Jenny **wish** that they **had received** fellowships
before they got to Stanford University.

WRONG: She wishes that she were a good daughter and never
disobeyed her parents.

RIGHT: . She **wishes** that she **had been** a good daughter and **had never disobeyed** her parents.

PRACTICE TEST

Test 1. SENTENCE COMPLETION: Choose the CORRECT answer.

1. We earnestly wish that we_____still young.

   A. are

   B. were

2. The little girl wishes that she_____a bird.

   A. were

   B. was

3. They wish that they_____more time with their children.

   A. had spent

   B. spend

4. We all wish that we_____the lottery.

   A. win

   B. won

5. I wish that I_____Helen at the University of Victoria.

A. had met

B. have met

Test 2. SENTENCE CORRECTION: Choose the INCORRECT word or phrase and CORRECT it.

1. I wish I know that beautiful girl's phone number

2. It rains a lot. I wish it doesn't rain so often in Vancouver.

3. The little girl often wishes that she is a bird.

4. I wish I know that Joyce was sick. I would have gone to see her.

5. Do you wish that you have studied business instead of science?

ANSWER KEY

Test 1:

1. B

2. A

3. A

4. B

5. A

Test 2:

1. I **wish** I **knew** that beautiful girl's phone number

2. It rains a lot. I **wish** it **didn't rain** so often in Vancouver.

3. The little girl often **wishes** that she **were** a bird.

4. I **wish** I **had known** that Joyce was sick. I would have gone to see her.

5. Do you **wish** that you **had studied** business instead of science?

CHAPTER 8

MODALS AND
MODAL-LIKE VERBS

LESSON 33

AFTER *WILL*, *WOULD*, OR OTHER MODALS, USE THE BASE FORM OF THE VERB CORRECTLY

ERROR EXAMPLE

WRONG: All of the books that you will need for this report can found in the library.

RIGHT: . All of the books that you will need for this report **can be found** in the library.

GRAMMAR POINT

The modal auxiliaries in English are *can, could, had better, may, might, must, ought (to), shall, should, will, would.*

In general, modals express that a speaker feels something is necessary, advisable, permissible, possible, or probable.

The following outlines the uses of verb forms after modals:

1. After all MODALS use the base form of the verb (V):

Henry **must go** to New York this weekend.

She **should pay** more attention to his research project.

We **had better leave** early so that we can catch the flight.

You **will have** to get his done by five o'clock this afternoon.

We **may choose** to write this exam in class or at home.

WRONG: According to Samson, his dog can recognizing English
               words.

RIGHT: . According to Samson, his dog **can recognize** English
               words.

WRONG: She had better to get prepared for her final examination.

RIGHT: . She **had better get** prepared for her final examination.

WRONG: If he had followed my advice, he wouldn't gone to a
               foreign country to find a job.

RIGHT: . If he had followed my advice, he **wouldn't have gone** to a foreign country to find a job.

2. Use the Past Participle after MODAL + HAVE:

I **should have** *applied* to Harvard University earlier.

She **must have** *got* his test result for the TOEFL.

Tom and Jessie **might have** *enjoyed* the party.

3. When we change direct speech to indirect speech, *could, would, should,* and *might* do not change form.

Direct Speech:

"You **should** always finish your homework on time."

Indirect Speech:

My supervisor said that **I should** always finish my homework on time.

4. Use *MUST HAVE* + Past Participle for past conclusion only:

The ground is wet, it **must have rained**.

It's almost midnight, Mary **must have gone** to sleep.

5. Use *HAD* + Infinitive for past obligation:

She **had to go** to see the doctor last night.

When we were poor, we **had to eat** grass in order to survive.

6. The MODAL *WOULD* is often combined with *like to* or *rather* to form a modal-like verb. Use *WOULD LIKE TO* to mean *want to*; use *WOULD RATHER* to mean *prefer to*:

I **would like to** go to the movie tonight.

I **would rather** go to the movie tonight than go to a party.

7. MODALS used in passive sentences must be followed by *be + Past Participle* of the main verb:

The woman who **could** *be identified* with her finger print was

arrested for theft at the airport.

The boy who **might *be punished*** for not doing his homework is actually a very good friend of mine.

PRACTICE TEST

Test 1. SENTENCE COMPLETION: Choose the CORRECT answer.

1. The bathroom is flooding. The pipes must_____.

    A. be broken

    B. have been broken

2. It_____last night because the ground is wet.

    A. rained

    B. must have rained

3. It is almost two o'clock in the morning. They must _____in New York.

    A. have arrived

    B. arrive

4. The girl who_____the next super model is actually a close friend of mine.

    A. ought to be

    B. might be

5. I_____to a community college at home than go to a big university abroad.

 A. would go

 B. would rather go

Test 2. SENTENCE CORRECTION: Choose the INCORRECT word or phrase and CORRECT it.

1. The room is empty; they left already.

2. Everybody does his duty.

3. We ought water the plants regularly.

4. Jack said that he will have gone to Stanford next year.

5. The movie will have begin by the time we get there.

Test 1:

1. B

2. B

3. A

4. B

5. B

Test 2:

1. The room is empty; they **must have left** already.

2. Everybody should do his duty.

3. We **must** water the plants regularly.

4. Jack said that he **might go** to Stanford next year.

5. The movie **will have begun** by the time we get there.

LESSON 34

LOGICAL CONCLUSIONS:

EVENTS IN THE PRESENT

ERROR EXAMPLE

WRONG: Me: "Fine, but I didn't pay the last time. They must do things differently down in the south."

RIGHT: Me: "Fine, but I didn't pay the last time. They **must be doing** things differently down in the south."

GRAMMAR POINT

When modal verb *must* is followed by auxiliary verb *have* + be + *ing* or an adjective, it expresses a logical conclusion based on evidence. The conclusion is about an event happening now. Remember that avoid using a verb in its original form instead of the -*ing* form.

We haven't heard from her for a long time. She **must be doing** well with her studies in Rochester.

Michael is on vacation in Las Vegas. He **must be having** a good time over there.

I called him several times but there was no answer. Jack **must be very busy** with his dissertation.

WRONG: The rich people must buy a lot of expensive cars now because the prices are going up.

RIGHT: The rich people **must be buying** a lot of expensive cars now because the prices are going up.

WRONG: I call her office several times, but there was no answer. She is busy now.

RIGHT: I call her office several times, but there was no answer. She **must be busy** now.

WRONG: Johnny has been in Beijing for about a week. We haven't heard from him yet. He must have a good time there.

RIGHT: Johnny has been in Beijing for about a week. We haven't heard from him yet. He **must be having** a good time there.

PRACTICE TEST

Test 1. SENTENCE COMPLETION: Choose the CORRECT answer.

1. I looked round and thought I _____..

   A. must do something wrong

   B. must be doing something wrong

2. Since the American buffalo has been removed from the endangered species list, it_____itself again.

   A. must reproduce

   B. must be reproducing

3. It is almost the end of the semester. The students_____for their final exams.

   A. must prepare

   B. must be preparing

4. The Hollywood actress is welcomed everywhere in the country. She_____very popular among the common people.

   A. must be

   B. must have been

5. Daniel has just got his first big pay check of ten thousand dollars. He_____all the way to the bank.

A. must sing

B. must be singing

Test 2. SENTENCE CORRECTION: Choose the INCORRECT word or phrase and CORRECT it.

1. The line is busy; someone should be using the telephone now.

2. Bob is absent; he must have been sick again (now).

3. He is taking a walk; he must have felt better now.

4. She must be study at the library now because all of her books are gone.

5. Sarah must get a divorce (now) because her husband is living in an apartment.

ANSWER KEY

Test 1:

1. B (**looked around and thought...must be doing**: logical conclusion based on evidence)

2. B (**since...has been removed...must be reproducing**: logical conclusion based on evidence)

3. B

4. A

5. B

Test 2:

1. The line is busy; someone **must be using** the telephone now.

2. Bob is absent; **he must be sick** again (now).

3. He is taking a walk; **he must be feeing** better now.

4. She **must be studying** at the library now because all of her books are gone.

5. Sarah **must be getting** a divorce (now) because her husband is living in an apartment.

LESSON 35

LOGICAL CONCLUSIONS:

EVENTS IN THE PAST

ERROR EXAMPLE

WRONG: Mary had high fever last night, she caught a very bad cold on her way home.

RIGHT: Mary had high fever last night, she **must have caught** a very bad cold on her way home.

GRAMMAR POINT

Remember that *must* is a modal verb. When *must* is followed by auxiliary verb *have* + Past Participle, it expresses a logical conclusion based on evidence. The conclusion is about an event happened in the past.

Helen has been staying at home most of the time. She **must have been fired** by her boss.

Professor Hoy seems to know almost anything. He **must have traveled** around the world or have read all the books in the library.

WRONG: When the weather becomes colder, we know that the air mass is originated in the Arctic rather than over the Gulf of Mexico.

RIGHT: When the weather becomes colder, we know that the air mass must **have been originated** in the Arctic rather than over the Gulf of Mexico.

WRONG: Michael knows a lot about local Japanese customs and habits. He must lived in Japan for a while.

RIGHT: Michael knows a lot about local Japanese customs and habits. He **must have lived** in Japan for a while.

PRACTICE TEST

Test 1. SENTENCE COMPLETION: Choose the CORRECT answer.

1. From the spunky look on his face you could tell he_____.

A. must have done well in the test.

B. must do well in the test.

2. Being on the list of 400 richest Americans, Douglas Cabinsky, the car dealer_____ .

A. must work very hard

B. must have worked very hard.

3. Douglas Mackey got every question right on the exam. He_____a lot of time preparing for it.

A. must spend

B. must have spent

4. They are back from the station. They_____the train.

A. must miss

B. must have missed

5. He lives in a huge mansion on the Westside. He_____big money in the oil crisis.

A. must have made

B. must be making

Test 2. SENTENCE CORRECTION: Choose the INCORRECT word or phrase and CORRECT it.

1. The streets are wet; it should have rained last night.

2. This pen won't write; it can have run out of ink (in the past).

3. The ring that I was looking at is gone; someone else must buy it.

4. He doesn't have his keys; he must locked them in his car.

5. I don't see Martha any where; she must be left early.

ANSWER KEY

Test 1:

1. A (**could tell…must have done:** logical reasoning and conclusion based on evidence)

2. B (**being** on…**must have worked:** logical conclusion based on evidence)

3. B

4. B

5. A

Test 2:

1. The streets are wet; it **must have rained** last night.

2. This pen won't write; it **must have run** out of ink (in the past).

3. The ring that I was looking at is gone; someone else **must have bought** it.

4. He doesn't have his keys; he **must have locked** them in his car.

5. I don't see Martha any where; she **must have left** early.

CHAPTER 9

MODIFIERS AND DANGLING PARTICIPLES

LESSON **36**

DANGLING MODIFIERS:

USE *-ING* AND *-ED* MODIFYING

PHRASES CORRECTLY

ERROR EXAMPLE

WRONG: Having won the world championship for swimming, the Chairman of the Olympic Committee presented the gold medal to the player.

RIGHT: **Having won** the world championship for swimming, the **player** was presented with a gold medal by the Chairman of the Olympic Committee.

GRAMMAR POINT

In English, *-ing* and *-ed* participles are used in phrases which modify the main clause. This structure, also known as a dangling modifier or dangling participle, is usually a *–ing* participial phrase or an *–ed* participial phrase, this phrase must be followed by a comma and then by the noun or pronoun that is performing the action conveyed by the participle.

Having hidden the new iPhone in her pocket, Mary left the room.

Running across the street, the little dog was hit by a car.

Sitting alone on a big rock in Cypress Mountain, Jennifer was

frightened to death by a strange noise.

In the first example, *Mary* performs the action of *having hidden the new iPhone*. In the second example, *the little dog* performs the action of *running across the street*. In the third example, *Jennifer* performs the action of *sitting alone on a big rock in Cypress Mountain.*

To understand more fully the use of the dangling modifiers, check out the following error examples:

WRONG: Wearing a sparkling red dress, the dog was led out for a walk by the little girl.

RIGHT: **Wearing** a sparkling red dress, **the little girl** led the dog out for a walk.

WRONG: Having finished our class, it was time for us to go home.

RIGHT: **Having finished** our class, **we thought** it was time to go home.

In the first error example, *the little girl* performs the action of *wearing the sparking red dress*. In the second error example, *we* perform the action of *finishing our class*.

PRACTICE TEST

Test 1. SENTENCE COMPLETION: Choose the CORRECT answer.

1. Having achieved these aims, _____.

    A. he sought to preserve a new European equilibrium through prudence and restraint

    B. a new European equilibrium through prudence and restraint was sought to preserve by him

2. The squirrel, _____, hid its nuts in a variety of places.

    A. tried to prepare for winter

    B. trying to prepare for winter

3. Wearing a red leather jacket, _____.

    A. the little cat was led out for a walk by Mary.

    B. Mary led the little cat out for a walk.

4. Having finished our exam, _____.

A. it was decided that we go out for a drink.

B. we decided to go out for a drink.

5. Running across the street, _____.

A. a taxi hit Jenny

B. Jenny was hit by a taxi

Test 2. SENTENCE CORRECTION: Choose the INCORRECT word or phrase and CORRECT it.

1. Having finished dinner, it was time to go to the movies.

2. Being left alone, it was very scary for me in a big house.

3. With its antlers weblike the feet of a duck, the North American moose is easy to identify.

4. Anyone interesting in the game can participate.

5. Seeing the business opportunity, a shopping mall was built here by George.

ANSWER KEY

Test 1:

1. A (**Having achieved…he sought to preserve**: here *he* is the

performer of both actions in the dangling participle and the main sentence)

2. B (**trying to prepare...hid**, the performer of both actions is the squirrel)

3. B

4. B

5. B

Test 2:

1. Having finished dinner, **we thought** it was time to go to the movies.

2. Being left alone, **I felt** it was very scary in a big house.

3. With its antlers **webbed like** the feet of a duck, the North American moose is easy to identify.

4. Anyone **interested** in the game can participate.

5. Seeing the business opportunity, **George** built a shopping mall here.

LESSON 37

MISPLACED MODIFIERS: POSITION ADJECTIVES AND ADVERBS CORRECTLY

ERROR EXAMPLE

WRONG: He began hosting sporadically bug dinner parties,

gatherings of friends and friends of friends.

RIGHT: He began **sporadically** hosting bug dinner parties,
gatherings of friends and friends of friends.

GRAMMAR POINT

In English, an adjective normally appears in front of the noun it modifies. For adverbs, it can appear in many positions, however, it can not come in between a verb and its object.

Michael studies **hard**.

Jack **hardly** studies.

We have received the most **recent** information about the election.

She said that she had something **very important** to tell us.

WRONG: I have news important to tell you tonight.

RIGHT: I have **important news** to tell you tonight.

WRONG: Jennifer is studying very hard French with the help of a
              private tutor from Paris.

RIGHT: Jennifer **is studying** French **very hard** with the help of a
              private tutor from Paris.

PRACTICE TEST

Test 1. SENTENCE COMPLETION: Choose the CORRECT answer.

1. He _____, when he felt his sickness departing, and became strong and healthy as in the days of his youth.

   A. had tasted scarcely it

   B. had scarcely tasted it

2. To share his expensive apartment downtown, Jacky_____.

   A. is desperately looking for a new roommate

   B. is looking for a new roommate desperately

3. There have been_____in the new admission agreement.

   A. dramatic changes

   B. changes dramatic

4. Jake mentioned that he had_____to tell us.

   A. highly confidential something

   B. something highly confidential

5. They were very surprised that I_____.

   A. was happy terribly not to accept the prize

   B. was terribly happy not to accept the prize

Test 2. SENTENCE CORRECTION: Choose the INCORRECT word or phrase and CORRECT it.

1. I only have one best friend in New York City.

2. She has bought just a new four-door Ford.

3. We thought it was importantly something we had to do.

4. Michael has been late terrible for class recently.

5. Is there anything with your computer wrong?

ANSWER KEY

Test 1:

1. B (had **scarcely** tasted it: never place an adverb in between a verb and its object.)

2. A (is **desperately** looking: never place an adverb in between a verb and its object.)

3. A

4. B

5. B

Test 2:

1. I have **only** one best friend in New York City.

2. She has **just** bought a new four-door Ford.

3. We thought it was something **important** we had to do.

4. Michael has been **terribly** late for class recently.

5. Is there anything **wrong** with your computer?

LESSON 38

USE *FEW* AND *A FEW*,

LITTLE AND *A LITTLE*,

MUCH AND *MANY* CORRECTLY

ERROR EXAMPLE

WRONG: When there is a few money remaining after all expenses have been paid, we say that a small economic surplus or profit has been created.

RIGHT: When there is **a little** money remaining after all expenses have been paid, we say that a small economic surplus or profit has been created.

GRAMMAR POINT

1. **The difference between** *few* **and** *a few* **is that** *few* **means not a lot,** *a few* **means some.** *Few, fewer, fewest,* **and** *a few* **must be followed by plural count nouns.**

There are **fewer** international **students** at the State University this year than last year.

The small ivy league university still has **a few** doctoral students from other countries.

WRONG: There is few water in the river during the dry season.

RIGHT: There is **little** water in the river during the dry season.

WRONG: Tom has the least friends among the students in his class.

RIGHT: Tom has **the fewest** friends among the students in his class.

2. **The difference between** *little* **and** *a little* **is that** *little* **means not a lot,** *a little* **means some.** *Little, less, least,* **and** *a little* **must be followed by uncount nouns.**

In the old days, parents gave **little** advice to their children about sex

and love.

Little information is currently available to researchers and physicians who study and treat acromegaly, a glandular disorder characterized by enlargement and obesity.

After paying the tuition, I had only **a little** money left for grocery.

WRONG: There is no many news about when the housing prices will drop in Vancouver.

RIGHT: There is **little** news about when the housing prices will drop in Vancouver.

WRONG: Though he is busy, he still has a few time for his children over the weekend.

RIGHT: Though he is busy, he still has **a little** time for his children over the weekend.

3. The difference between *much* and *many* is that *much* modifies uncount nouns and *many* modifies count nouns. Both *much* and *many* mean a lot.

Her parents didn't have **much knowledge** about economics.

We have **many** foreign **graduates** working in the high-tech industry in Silicon Valley.

Too **much information** is sometimes a dangerous thing in our life.

WRONG: There was too many traffic in the old school district.

RIGHT: There was **too much** traffic in the old school district.

WRONG: She had so many homework that she couldn't go on a date.

RIGHT: She had **so much** homework that she couldn't go on a date.

PRACTICE TEST

Test 1. SENTENCE COMPLETION: Choose the CORRECT answer.

1. We had_____food to eat when we were poor.

   A. few

   B. little

2. There was only_____water left in the house.

   A. a few

   B. a little

3. Even with the development of science and technology, we still
   have_____knowledge about the aliens.

   A. much

   B. little

4. There has been_____noise around town that there might
   be an earthquake here in about a hundred year's time.

   A. too much

   B. to many

5. Since he left for the Africa, we have had
   very_____information about where he is.

   A. little

B. few

Test 2. SENTENCE CORRECTION: Choose the INCORRECT word or phrase and CORRECT it.

1. Give me little butter, please.

2. We have a little news about the plane crash.

3. There are few tickets left for the concert.

4. A few people in my apartment building are friendly.

5. She can speak so much languages fluently.

ANSWER KEY

Test 1:

1. B

2. B

3. B

4. A

5. A

Test 2:

1. Give me **a little** butter, please.

2. We have **little news** about the plane crash.

3. There are **a few tickets** left for the concert.

4. **Few people** in my apartment building are friendly.

5. She can speak so **many languages** fluently.

CHAPTER 10

PRONOUNS AND PRONOUN REFERENCES

LESSON 39

USE PRONOUNS CORRECTLY

ERROR EXAMPLE

WRONG: "Everybody should weigh their words very carefully. What
we do not need is alarm in financial markets," she said

RIGHT: "Everybody should weigh **his** words very carefully. What
we do not need is alarm in financial markets," she said

GRAMMAR POINT

Pronouns are used to replace or refer to nouns, gerunds, infinitives, and sometimes entire clauses. Pronouns change form depending on their functions in sentences.

Remember that always check personal, possessive, and reflexive pronouns for agreement.

They are the offspring of a great family from Ireland.

It is **our** duty to serve and protect the people.

Jennifer is a very close friend of **ours**.

We ourselves are short of supplies because of the storm.

Michael has just got **his** degree in economics from Cambridge University.

The pretty girl doesn't allow anybody to see **her** nor does **she** allow anyone to fall in love with **her**.

WRONG: Nobody should be judged by their appearance.

RIGHT: Nobody should be judged by **his** appearance.

WRONG: We must let all citizens know his rights and obligations in the society.

RIGHT: We must let all citizens know **their** rights and obligations in the society.

PRACTICE TEST

Test 1. SENTENCE COMPLETION: Choose the CORRECT answer.

1. Everyone must sign_____at the reception desk.

    A. their name

    B. his name

2. He is one of those people who always_____.

    A. brag about themselves

    B. brag about himself

3. Everyone is responsible for _____own personal safety.

    A. their

    B. his

4. When you live alone off campus, you have learn how to take care
of_____.

    A. yourselves

    B. yourselfs

5. They have decided to paint their apartment_____.

    A. theirselves

    B. themselves

Test 2. SENTENCE CORRECTION: Choose the INCORRECT word or phrase and CORRECT it.

1. Between you and I, the economic situation does not look bad.

2. It was him who knocked on the door last night.

3. Jack is as tall as me.

4. You don't have to worry about me. I can cook myself my dinner.

5. It is she, the one whom nobody likes.

ANSWER KEY

Test 1:

1.B (Here **everyone** is the third person singular, therefore, the possessive pronoun should be *his*.)

2. A (Here you should use reflexive pronoun **themselves** because it refers to *people*.)

3. B

4. A

5. B

Test 2:

1. Between you and **me**, the economic situation does not look bad.

2. It was **he** who knocked on the door last night.

3. Jack is as tall as **I.**

4. You don't have to worry about me. I can cook dinner **myself.**

5. It is **her**, the one whom nobody likes.

LESSON 40

USE REFLEXIVE

PRONOUNS CORRECTLY

ERROR EXAMPLE

WRONG: The best ones can take a good idea and use it to transform itself from embryos into giants in a few years, as Amazon and Google have.

RIGHT: The best ones can take a good idea and use it to transform **themselves** from embryos into giants in a few years, as Amazon and Google have.

GRAMMAR POINT

In English, a reflexive pronoun (*myself, ourselves, yourself, yourselves, himself, herself, themselves, itself*) can be used as the complement of a sentence or a clause. It can also be used as the object of a preposition.

After saving for his whole life, Michael finally built **himself** a huge mansion in the Fraser Valley.

Mary is not quite **herself** today.

He fixed the car **himself**.

They divided the prize among **themselves**.

WRONG: When you take a test, you should always give you enough time to check the answers before you hand it in.

RIGHT: When you take a test, you should always give **yourself** enough time to check the answers before you hand it in.

WRONG: It seems everyone knows favoritism exists — but nobody wants to put his hand up and say he is guilty of it itself.

RIGHT: It seems everyone knows favoritism exists — but nobody wants to put his hand up and say he is guilty of it **himself**.

PRACTICE TEST

Test 1. SENTENCE COMPLETION: Choose the CORRECT answer.

1. According to the Fifth Amendment to the U.S. Constitution,

nobody should be compelled to be a witness_____.

A. against themselves

B. against himself

2. All this would be apart from the failure of two generations of efforts to build a strong European framework_____.

A. around Germany themselves.

B. around Germany itself.

3. She said that she would finish the research project_____.

A. by herself

B. for herself

4. Bad memories will not go away_____.

A. theirselves

B. of themselves

5. What has happened behind the closed doors is _____.

A. between themselves

B. themselves

Test 2. SENTENCE CORRECTION: Choose the INCORRECT word or phrase and CORRECT it.

1. Be careful with these sharp tools or you will hurt to you.

2. A child can usually feed self by the age of six months.

3. Since nobody knew how to swim in my family, I had to teach me how to swim.

4. Help you to whatever you like, it is free.

5. A modern microwave that can clean it is really unbelievable.

ANSWER KEY

Test 1:

1. B (Here **nobody** is the third person singular, therefore, *itself* should be used here.)

2. B (Here **Germany** is the third person singular, therefore, *itself* should be used here.)

3. A

4. B

5. A

Test 2:

1. Be careful with these sharp tools or you will hurt **yourself**.

2. A child can usually feed **himself** by the age of six months.

3. Since nobody knew how to swim in my family, I had to teach **myself** how to swim.

4. Help **yourself** to whatever you like, it is free.

5. A modern microwave that can clean **itself** is really unbelievable.

LESSON 41

CHECK PRONOUN REFERENCE FOR AGREEMENT

ERROR EXAMPLE

WRONG: And when it comes to fathering healthy children, older men, it turns out, are just as much at the mercy of its biological clocks as women.

RIGHT: And when it comes to fathering healthy children, older **men**, it turns out, are just as much at the mercy of **their** biological clocks as women.

GRAMMAR POINT

A pronoun must clearly refer to the noun or noun phrase for which it substitutes. Remember that every pronoun or possessive agrees with the noun or noun phrase it refers to in number and in person.

Since you can clean the room **yourself**, why do you have to pay to hire somebody else to do it?

Everyone should always bear in mind that he is always responsible for **himself** and the society.

WRONG: When children experience too much frustration, its behavior ceases to be integrated.

RIGHT:　When **children** experience too much frustration, **their** behavior ceases to be integrated.

WRONG: Mary paid more attention to her dog than its baby girl.

RIGHT:　**Mary** paid more attention to her dog than **her** baby girl.

WRONG:. The committee and their members all voted in his favor.

RIGHT:　The **committee** and **its** members all voted in his favor.

PRACTICE TEST

Test 1. SENTENCE COMPLETION: Choose the CORRECT answer.

1. It seems everyone knows favoritism exists — but nobody wants to put _____.

   A. their hand up and say he is guilty of it himself.

   B. his hand up and say he is guilty of it himself.

2. Although the destruction that_____is often terrible, cyclones

   benefit a much wider belt than they devastate.

   A. they cause

   B. it causes

3. Those who come early can help_____with some coffee
   and donuts.

   A. itself

   B. themselves

4. Nobody is allowed to leave this room without
   finishing_____exam.

   A. his

   B. their

5. If the students decide to take the reading break next week, they
   have to get the permission_____supervisors.

   A. from its

   B. their

Test 2. SENTENCE CORRECTION: Choose the INCORRECT word or phrase and CORRECT it.

1. Nobody should be judged by their appearance.

2. We must let all citizens know his rights and obligations in the society.

3. He is one of those people who always brag about himself.

4. The current world situation gives the rich country more opportunities than the poor countries.

5. The students are trying their best to help the classmates in need.

ANSWER KEY

Test 1:

1. B (**nobody   his**)

2. A (**they   cyclones**)

3. B

4. A

5. B

Test 2:

1. **Nobody** should be judged by **his** appearance.

2. We must let all **citizens** know **their** rights and obligations in the society.

3. He is one of those **people** who always brag about **themselves**.

4. The current world situation gives the **rich countries** more opportunities than the **poor countries**.

5. The _students are trying their best to help **their** classmates in need.

CHAPTER 11

VERBALS

LESSON 42

ERRORS WITH VERBALS

ERROR EXAMPLE

WRONG: It was the task of all interesting nations to make sure this new state of affairs did not spill over into tension – or worse.

RIGHT: It was the task of all **interested** nations to make sure this new state of affairs did not spill over into tension – or worse.

GRAMMAR POINT

Verbals are participles, gerunds, and infinitives. The following are the various kinds of uses of verbals:

1. **Participles can be used as adjectives. For present participles, they end with** *–ing*; **for past participles, they end with** *–ed*. **When modifying nouns, present participles tend to have active meaning whereas past participles have passive meaning.**

She is rumoured to be a **living** dictionary. (Present Participle)

The **damaged** car was finally repaired. (Past Participle)

WRONG: The millionaire's stealing Land Rover was finally recovered with the help of the police.

RIGHT: The millionaire's **stolen** Land Rover was finally recovered with the help of the police.

WRONG: The woman put the cleaning cups on the table.

RIGHT: The woman put the **cleaned** cups on the table.

2. **Gerunds are verbal nouns. They end in** *–ing* **like the present participle. They can be used as the subjects of verbs, the objects of prepositions and verbs like the following:**

admit	*deny*	*postpone*
appreciate	*enjoy*	*practice*
avoid	*finish*	*stop*

cannot help	*keep*	*suggest*
consider		

She has finished **reading** all the required books for the exam.

You must avoid **making** this kind of mistakes again.

Mary really enjoyed **meeting** her new roommates.

WRONG: Young people should always look forward to see miracles happen in their lives.

RIGHT: Young people should always look forward to **seeing** miracles happen in their lives.

WRONG: Jack denied to commit the crime.

RIGHT: Jack denied **committing** the crime.

The following verb phrases (verb + prepositions) can be followed by the gerund (V +ing):

be accustomed to	*decide on*	*plan on*
be interested in	*get through*	*put off*
be opposed to	*keep on*	*think about*
be used to	*look forward to*	*think of*

She was used to **living** in the country

We are looking forward to **seeing** you in Dallas.

If you keep on **practicing,** you will get a higher score on the exam.

I am thinking of **going** back to Hong Kong.

1. **Infinitives are formed with *to* plus the simple form of the verb. They can be used as the subjects of verbs and the objects of verbs like the following:**

agree	*forbid*	*mean*
care	*forget*	*offer*
decide	*hope*	*plan*
deserve	*intend*	*pretend*
fail	*learn*	*refuse*

He has agreed **to go** swimming with me.

We intend **to hold** the biggest celebration party ever.

Mary failed **to attend** the seminar on Saturday.

The secretary offered **to come** in early.

WRONG: John Glenn was the first American orbiting the Earth.

RIGHT: John Glenn was the first American **to orbit** the Earth.

WRONG: She has agreed to consider to quit smoking.

RIGHT: She has agreed to consider **quitting** smoking.

PRACTICE TEST

Test 1. SENTENCE COMPLETION: Choose the CORRECT answer.

1. The exhausting basketball players were too tired to move after they
   had won the championship.

   A. exhausting

   B. exhausted

2. Tenants of this building are advised to shut the windows in winter;
   for we_____.

   A. can not afford heating the outside

   B. can not afford to heat the outside

3. Nobody can afford_____the outside during the winter.

   A. heating

   B. to heat

4. Unfortunately, Mary failed_____to the convocation on
   time.

A. coming

B. to come

5. Michael definitely deserved_____a raise this year.

A. to get

B. getting

Test 2. SENTENCE CORRECTION: Choose the INCORRECT word or phrase and CORRECT it.

1. This new sports car is very easy driving.

2. The most important discovery knowing to all might be DNA.

3. No rich person can afford feeding such a hungry nation after the war.

4. Have finished dinner, we took a walk along the Thames.

5. No one looks forward to hear bad news after the college entrance exam.

ANSWER KEY

Test 1:

1. B (Here **exhausted** should be used because it is a past participle used as an adjective and it has a passive meaning.)

2. B (Here after *afford*, an infinitive **to heat** must be used instead of a gerund.)

3. B

4. B

5. A

Test 2:

1. This new sports car is very easy **to drive.**

2. The most important discovery **known** to all might be DNA.

3. No rich person can afford *to* **feed** such a hungry nation after the war.

4. **Having finished** dinner, we took a walk along the Thames.

5. No one looks forward to **hearing** bad news after the college entrance exam.

LESSON **43**

PROBLEMS WITH INFINITIVES

ERROR EXAMPLE

WRONG: For example, if we decide to play blackjack, the first thing
doing is decide how much we are going to wager or risk.

RIGHT: For example, if we decide to play blackjack, the first thing
to do is decide how much we are going to wager or risk.

GRAMMAR POINT

Infinitives are formed with *to* plus the simple form of the verb. They can
be used as the subjects of verbs and the objects of certain verbs.

We don't want you **to pretend** to know everything.

Jackson deserved **to be promoted** as the president of the company.

She forgot **to bring** her ticket to the movie.

We don't mean **to offend** you at all.

WRONG: Johnny got lost in New York City because he forgot
reading the direction on the tourist map.

RIGHT: Johnny got lost in New York City because he forgot

to read the direction on the tourist map.

Infinitives can be used as adjective phrases after noun phrases.

The next plane **to arrive** from New York is at midnight.

Jenny is lucky. She has a brother **to help her** whenever she needs it.

WRONG: Jack Daniel was the only man receiving this privilege

RIGHT: Jack Daniel was the only man **to receive** this privilege.

Infinitives can also be used to show purpose.

WRONG: He is learning Chinese for finding a job in China.

RIGHT: He is learning Chinese **to find** a job in China.

PRACTICE TEST

Test 1. SENTENCE COMPLETION: Choose the CORRECT answer.

1. The first man_____on the moon was Neil Armstrong.

   A. landing

   B. to land

2. _____on the college entrance test, we must study hard and be fully prepared.

   A. To get a higher score

   B. Getting a higher score

3. Jennifer is always the first person_____to the office to get my coffee ready in the morning.

   A. to come

   B. coming

4. We will talk about it at our next meeting_____next Monday.

   A. to be held

B. to hold

5. No one is entitled_____more than what he deserves in life.

    A. receiving

    B. to receive

Test 2. SENTENCE CORRECTION: Choose the INCORRECT word or phrase and CORRECT it.

1. She is reputed to be a spy for KGB during the Cold War.

2. The injured worker was reported to die the day before.

3. They chose to not have attended the meeting.

4. Our job is help you to pass the standardized exam.

5. The police officer offered give her a ride home because she was drunk.

ANSWER KEY

Test 1:

1. B (Here we use infinitive **to land** instead of the present participle *landing* because *to land on the moon* functions as an adjective phrase to modify the noun before it.)

2. A (here an infinitive **to get**... must be used as the adverbial of purpose)

3. A

4. A

5. B

Test 2:

1. She is reputed **to have been** a spy for the KGB during the Cold War.

2. The injured worker was reported **to have died** the day before.

3. They chose **not to attend** the meeting.

4. Our job is **to help** you to pass the standardized exam.

5. The police officer offered **to give** her a ride home because she was drunk.

CHAPTER 12

COMPARATIVES

AND SUPERLATIVES

LESSON 44

ERRORS WITH COMPARATIVES

AND SUPERLATIVES

ERROR EXAMPLE

WRONG: Perhaps more than any place in Asia, Hong Kong's energy comes from a powerful relationship with the present.

RIGHT: Perhaps more than **any other** place in Asia, Hong Kong's energy comes from a powerful relationship with the present.

GRAMMAR POINT

There are three kinds of comparison in English. They are the equative, comparative, and the superlative.

Equative degree is used to show equality.

This building is **as** tall **as** that one.

This building is **the same** height **as** that one.

WRONG: This building is as tall like that one by the seaside.

RIGHT: This building is **as** tall **as** that one by the seaside.

WRONG: Although we often use "speed" and "velocity" interchangeably, in a technical sense, "speed" is not always as "velocity".

RIGHT: Although we often use "speed" and "velocity" interchangeably, in a technical sense, "speed" is not always **the same as** "velocity.".

The comparative degree is used to compare two things that are not equal. In your test, when you see the word *more*, look for *than*.

To use comparatives correctly, pay special attention to the following rules:

1. One syllable or two syllable adjectives ending in –y, change the –y to –i before adding –er.

Susan is busy, but her mother is even **busier**.

She is pretty, but her sister is **prettier**.

WRONG: When you are happy, I am more happier.

RIGHT: When you are happy, I am **happier**.

2. We put *more* before the adjective if it has two or three syllables to form the comparative.

Tom is handsome, but his brother is **more handsome**.

Life in the country is enjoyable, but life in the city is **more enjoyable.**

WRONG: She looks gorgeous, but her younger sister looks the most gorgeous.

RIGHT: She looks gorgeous, but her younger sister looks more gorgeous.

3. Remember that *than* is the only structure word that can follow comparatives.

This tree is definitely **taller than** that one.

Jennifer is **more trustworthy than** her big sister.

WRONG: Michael is definitely more smarter than Jack Daniels.

RIGHT: Michael is definitely **smarter** than Jack Daniels.

The superlative degree is used to compare three or more things that are not equal. When you see the words like *one of the*, look for *most* or a word ending in *–est*.

To use superlatives correctly, pay special attention to the following rules:

1. One syllable or two syllable adjectives ending in –*y*, change the –*y* to –*est* .

Jack is taller than Michael, but Jordan is the **tallest**.

Jack is stronger than Michael, but Jordan is **the strongest**.

2. We put *the most* before the adjective if it has two or three syllables to form the superlative.

Joyce is more charming than Lucy, but Helen is the **most charming**.

Vancouver is one of the **most beautiful** cities in the world.

WRONG: One of the most exciting thing for parents is a baby's first word spoken like a miracle..

RIGHT: **One of** the most exciting **things** for parents is a baby's first word spoken like a miracle.

PRACTICE TEST

Test 1. SENTENCE COMPLETION: Choose the CORRECT answer.

1. Vancouver is more beautiful_____ in the world.

   A. than any city

   B. than any other city

2. He is the _____person in the class to be late.

   A. least possible

   B. less possible

3. Jenny Jackson, our college flower, is_____ _____girl on campus.

   A. more beautiful than any

   B. more beautiful than any other

4. Between the twin brothers, Thomas is_____.

   A. the tallest

   B. the taller of the two

5. The City of Victoria is_____in the world.

   A. the most livable city

   B. more livable than any other cities

Test 2. SENTENCE CORRECTION: Choose the INCORRECT word or phrase and CORRECT it.

1. Our building is the same height like yours.

2. Jennifer is definitely smart as Marilyn.

3. The population of my hometown is much smaller than Shanghai.

4. The higher the degree you have, the more high wage you will get.

5. One of the most difficult problem in math is logical reasoning.

ANSWER KEY

Test 1:

1. B (Here you should use **than any other** *city* instead of *than any city* because any city includes Vancouver itself.)

2. A (Here you should use **least** because there must be at least three or more students in a class.)

3. B

4. B

5. A

Test 2:

1. Our building is **the same** height **as** yours.

2. Jennifer is definitely **as** smart **as** Marilyn.

3. The population of my hometown is much smaller than **that of** Shanghai.

4. The higher the degree you have, the **higher** the wage you will get.

5. One of the most difficult **problems** in math is logical reasoning.

LESSON 45

COMPARATIVE ESTIMATES:

USE *MORE THAN* AND

LESS THAN CORRECTLY

ERROR EXAMPLE

WRONG: After the last summit the financial markets' enthusiasm over the ludicrous idea of a leveraged EFSF evaporated after fewer than 48 hours.

RIGHT: After the last summit the financial markets' enthusiasm over the ludicrous idea of a leveraged EFSF evaporated after **less than** 48 hours.

GRAMMAR POINT

More than or *less than* is used before a specific number to express an estimate that may be a little more or a little less than the number.

We have **more than** a hundred students signed up for the game..

Less than half of the seniors like the idea of going a trip abroad during the winter time.

WRONG: Nancy has more than twenty apartments downtown, but she has few than ten thousand dollars in her bank account.

RIGHT: Nancy has more than twenty apartments downtown, but she has **less than** ten thousand dollars in her bank account.

WRONG: He has a lot than ten cars to choose from in his garage.

RIGHT: He has **more than** ten cars to choose from in his garage.

PRACTICE TEST

Test 1. SENTENCE COMPLETION: Choose the CORRECT answer.

1. He said that the company had_____, but he declined to comment further.

   A. more than a hundred employee

   B. more than a hundred employees

2. In the Longwood Garden, you can see_____a thousand

   kinds of flowers and exotic plants.

   A. more than

   B. many

3. After a whole night of blast in the bar, Jackson had_____

   A.. less than five dollars left in his pocket

   B. fewer than five dollars left in his pocket

4. The billionaire has_____twenty luxury cars in his garage.

   A. a lot than

   B. more than

5. We have_____half of the population on our side in this Presidential election; therefore, we will win.

   A. more than

   B. much more than

Test 2. SENTENCE CORRECTION: Choose the INCORRECT word or phrase and CORRECT it.

1. More one hundred people came to the meeting.

2. We have lived in the United States for as less than seven years.

3. The main library has more as one million volumes.

4. A new shopping center on the north side will have five hundred shops more than.

5. There are most than fifty students in the lab, but only two computers.

ANSWER KEY

Test 1:

1. B (Here you should use **employees** instead of *employee* because after more than + a specific number, you should the plural noun.)

2. A (here **more than** should be used because we have a specific number *a thousand kinds*)

3. A

4. B

5. A

Test 2:

1. **More than one hundred** people came to the meeting.

2. We have lived in the United States for **less than seven years**.

3. The main library has **more than one million** volumes.

4. A new shopping center on the north side will have **more than five hundred** shops.

5. There are **more than fifty** students in the lab, but only two computers.

ACKNOWLEDGEMENTS

The author would like to thank his colleagues and students for their invaluable assistance in bringing this book to life.

The author and publisher are grateful to those who have made this publication possible by providing all kinds of support from editing, graphic design, and proof-reading. Efforts have been made to identify the source of materials used in this book, however, it has not always been possible to identify the sources of all the materials used, or to trace the copyright holders. If any omissions are brought to our attention, we will be happy to include the appropriate acknowledgements on reprinting.

ABOUT THE AUTHOR

Richard Lee is a professor of English and distinguished publishing scholar with more than twenty books published under his name. His books are available on Amazon, other online stores, and in bookstores worldwide. He pursued his doctoral education at the University of Rochester in New York and the University of British Columbia and received his Ph.D. in English. Dr. Lee lives in beautiful Vancouver, British Columbia.

24802190R00155

Made in the USA
Lexington, KY
01 August 2013